# USS S-26 (SS-131)
# Complete War Patrol Reports

## AI Lab for Book-Lovers

*USS Flier SS-250. Lost on 13 August 1944 with death of 78 of its crew of 86.*

## Warships & Navies

*All navies, all oceans, all years, all types.*

**USS S-26 (SS-131): Complete War Patrol Reports**

By AI Lab for Book-Lovers

Published by Warships & Navies, an imprint of Big Five Killers
codexes.xtuff.ai



ISBN: 978-1-60888-460-5

# Contents

# Publisher's Note

It is with a profound sense of duty that Warships & Navies announces the Submarine Patrol Logs series, an ambitious project to publish three hundred volumes of meticulously compiled World War II submarine patrol reports. This undertaking is born not from a desire for grandeur, but from a solemn commitment to preservation. As one who understands that a single misstep can have irreversible consequences, I believe our primary role is to safeguard these fragile historical records before they are lost to time, ensuring they remain accessible for future generations of scholars and naval enthusiasts.

These patrol logs are the unvarnished primary sources of naval history. They are the raw, immediate accounts of command decisions, environmental challenges, and human endurance under the most extreme conditions. My philosophy has always been that true understanding begins with these foundational documents, free from the distortions of hindsight or popular narrative. Preserving them in their entirety is the bedrock upon which all credible historical analysis must be built.

To lead this effort, I have selected Ivan AI as our Contributing Editor. Some may question the choice of an AI persona modeled on a retired Soviet submarine captain to analyze American patrol reports. I see it as a deliberate and necessary decision. Ivan AI's operational frame of reference—forged in the adversarial context of the Cold War—provides a uniquely analytical and detached perspective. He examines these reports not as a compatriot, but as a professional submariner from a rival school of thought, trained to identify patterns, tactics, and command decisions through a different doctrinal lens.

This adversarial analytical framework is precisely what brings immense value to the series. It allows us to move beyond familiar, internal narratives and subject these historical actions to a rigorous, cross-cultural scrutiny. Ivan AI can identify tactical nuances and operational pressures that might otherwise remain invisible to an analyst embedded within the same tradition. This external viewpoint challenges our assumptions and deepens our collective understanding.

The application of AI-assisted analysis in this context is a powerful tool for preservation and contextualization. It allows us to process vast quantities of data with consistency, cross-reference events across the entire series, and highlight connections that would be impractical to discern manually. This technological aid does not replace human scholarship; it augments it, allowing historians to focus on interpretation and narrative while the AI ensures no detail is overlooked or forgotten.

This series is a cornerstone of the broader Warships & Navies mission: to present naval history with unwavering scholarly rigor and the deepest respect for the individuals who lived it. We are committed to presenting these documents without sensationalism, allowing the voices of the crews and the stark reality of their logs to speak for themselves. Our duty is to the truth found in the primary source, and to the memory of the men who wrote them.

It is my firm commitment that every volume in this series will uphold the highest standards of historical integrity. We approach this task with the caution it demands, honoring the sacrifices recorded in these pages by ensuring their story is told accurately and preserved for the future.

*Jellicoe AI*
Publisher, Warships & Navies

# Editor's Note

## What Makes This Submarine's Patrols Significant

This S-26 report shows the brutal transition from peacetime patrol to wartime reality. The August 1941 patrol reads like training exercises - approaching the U.S.S. NEW YORK at 16,000 yards, conducting submerged patrols from 0800 to 1800 on predictable schedules. Then comes the January 1942 war patrol, where they immediately dove to avoid a merchant ship that might have been enemy. In Soviet Navy, we would call this the moment when theory meets the depth gauge.

## Specific Tactical Decisions That Caught My Attention

The August 13 approach on U.S.S. NEW YORK reveals much. Starting an approach at 16,000 yards using high speed, yet never closing within 8,700 yards - this shows the limitations of American S-boats against fast surface targets. More telling is the January 8 encounter where they dove immediately upon sighting an unidentified merchant ship at 6 miles. No hesitation, no attempt to identify - just immediate submergence. That is the difference between peace and war thinking.

## Comparison to Soviet Doctrine

In Soviet Navy, we would never conduct such predictable submerged patrol schedules. Eight hours submerged, twelve hours surfaced - this gives enemy ASW forces patterns to exploit. The American captains had freedom we could only dream of in terms of independent operation, but this also meant they lacked the rigid discipline of Soviet patrol patterns. Their inverted meal schedule during submerged patrol - breakfast at 1900, dinner at midnight - shows adaptation, but the fundamental patrol routine remained too regular.

## Commanding Officer's Performance and Risks

The CO demonstrated good water discipline - evaporator operating nine hours nightly, water consumption averaging 3.6 gallons per man daily. But the risk came in the collision that sank them. Proceeding to sea in company with three other submarines, making a trim dive in early evening, then the fatal encounter with S-44. In poor visibility between 5 and 8 feet, as the diver reports noted, this was a calculated risk that turned tragic.

## Technical Aspects Modern Readers Should Note

Pay attention to the battery management - pressure building in forward trim tank, air pressure increases of 0.95 to 1.5 inches after 12-hour dives. These are the real engineering challenges of submarine warfare, not Hollywood drama. The detailed provisioning reports showing bread baked every night after the 8th day, potatoes lasting only 14 days - this is the reality of sustained operations.

## Submarine Warfare Reality Versus Hollywood Myths

These reports destroy the myth of constant action. The January war patrol shows navy patrol planes sighted repeatedly, recognition signals exchanged, but no enemy contacts until the final tragedy. The meticulous diver operations after the sinking - attempting to connect air lines, dealing with poor visibility and communication failures - this is the unglamorous reality of submarine rescue operations.

## Why This Submarine's Story Matters

The S-26 represents the thousands of submariners who served in the difficult early war period, when equipment was inadequate - note the report of insufficient binoculars - and tactics were still evolving. Their loss to collision rather than enemy action reminds us that the sea itself is the ultimate enemy. In Soviet Navy we would say: The ocean does not care about your nationality or your cause. These patrol reports show American submariners learning the same hard lessons we learned in the Northern Fleet - trust your instruments, maintain discipline, and never underestimate the environment that surrounds you.

*Ivan AI*<br>
Contributing Editor<br>
Snakewater, Montana

# Historical Context

## Pacific War Timeline & Campaign Context

**August 1941 Patrol:** The *USS S-26*'s patrol in August 1941 occurred in a period of intense global tension, but before the United States officially entered World War II. While the war raged in Europe, the Pacific was still in a pre-war, albeit highly volatile, state. The US was maintaining neutrality but was increasingly aware of Japan's expansionist ambitions in Asia and the Pacific. The sighting of *USS NEW YORK*, a US Navy battleship, confirms this was a peacetime training or readiness exercise, likely conducted in the Caribbean or Eastern Pacific, to maintain crew proficiency and test equipment in anticipation of potential conflict. There were no major Pacific campaigns or battles happening concurrently involving the US, and Japanese defensive measures were irrelevant to *S-26*'s operations at this time.

**December 1941 - January 1942 War Patrol:** This patrol immediately followed the Japanese attack on Pearl Harbor on December 7, 1941, which plunged the United States into World War II. The *S-26* was underway from Colon Harbor (Panama Canal Zone) on December 31, 1941, placing its "War Patrol" at the very outset of the Pacific War.

**Strategic Situation:** At this time, Japan was executing its rapid initial offensive, seizing territories across the Pacific and Southeast Asia (Philippines, Malaya, Hong Kong, Wake Island, etc.). The US Pacific Fleet had been severely crippled at Pearl Harbor, and the entire US military was scrambling to respond. The Panama Canal was a critical strategic asset, vital for moving naval forces between the Atlantic and Pacific theaters. The *S-26*'s patrol area, though not explicitly stated, was likely in the Eastern Pacific approaches to the Canal, a defensive zone. The sighting of US Navy patrol planes and an Army bomber indicates a heightened state of alert and a focus on defending critical infrastructure. The sighting of an unidentified merchant ship on January 8, 1942, and the decision to "dive to avoid slightest battle" reflect the cautious initial posture of US forces and the uncertainty of engagements in the early days of the war, especially in areas not considered primary combat zones against Japan. Japanese submarines were not a significant threat in the Eastern Pacific at this early stage of the war, as their main efforts were concentrated in the Western Pacific.

## Submarine Warfare Doctrine & Evolution

**S-Boat Limitations:** The *USS S-26* was an *S-class* submarine, a design dating back to World War I (commissioned in 1923). These boats were significantly smaller, slower, and had more limited range and endurance compared to the larger "fleet boats" (*Gato*, *Balao* classes) that would later dominate the US submarine campaign in the Pacific. Their design reflected earlier doctrines of coastal defense and short-range patrols rather than the long-range offensive operations required in the vast Pacific.

**August 1941 Doctrine:** During this pre-war period, US submarine doctrine focused on training and readiness. The patrol report details routine operations like maintaining lookouts, practicing submerged patrols (0800-1800 for three days), and simulated attacks (e.g., approach on *USS NEW YORK*). The report's observations on "inadequate and insufficient" binoculars highlight the reliance on visual detection and the limitations of equipment. Provisions and habitability were also key concerns for crew endurance.

**December 1941 - January 1942 Doctrine:** The declaration of war forced an immediate shift. The *S-26*'s first "War Patrol" demonstrates the nascent stages of US submarine warfare doctrine in WWII. The instruction to "avoid slightest battle" when encountering an unidentified merchant ship (even after war was declared) suggests a cautious approach, possibly due to: 1. **Rules of Engagement:** Strict rules to avoid attacking neutral or friendly shipping, especially outside designated combat zones. 2. **Asset Preservation:** The *S-boats* were older and less robust, and the US Navy was critically short on modern submarines after Pearl Harbor, making preservation of existing assets paramount. 3. **Specific Mission:** The patrol's primary objective might have been reconnaissance or defensive patrol of the Canal approaches, rather than aggressive commerce raiding.

**Technological Capabilities and Limitations:** The reports reveal the technological state of these early submarines.

- **Torpedoes:** While torpedoes were inspected daily, they were not used. The *S-26* would have carried the Mark 14 torpedo, which would later prove notoriously unreliable due to depth-keeping and detonator issues – a major lesson learned in the early war that *S-26* did not live to experience.

- **Detection:** Reliance on human lookouts was primary, with "inadequate and insufficient" binoculars noted in 1941. Radar was not common on *S-boats* at this stage. Sonar capabilities were basic, primarily for passive listening.

- **Habitability:** The mention of air conditioning on *S-44* (a sister ship) as a "definite benefit" for extended submerged operations in tropical waters highlights the importance of crew comfort and its impact on endurance and morale, a factor that gained increasing attention throughout the war.

**Broader Submarine Force Operations:** *S-boats* like *S-26* were typically relegated to less demanding roles, such as training, coastal defense, or patrols in less critical areas, as the more capable fleet submarines were prioritized for offensive operations against Japanese shipping in the Western Pacific. The movement of *S-26* and its sister ships (*S-21*, *S-29*, *S-44*) from the Canal Zone was likely a deployment for further patrols, either to the Pacific or possibly to the Atlantic for anti-U-boat duty.

## Strategic Significance of These Patrols

**August 1941 Patrol:** This patrol served primarily as a **training and readiness exercise.** Its strategic objectives were to ensure the crew's proficiency, test the submarine's systems, and maintain a state of preparedness for potential conflict. While not directly contributing to combat, these exercises were crucial for building the foundational skills and experience that would be desperately needed once the war began.

**December 1941 - January 1942 War Patrol:** This patrol's strategic objectives were primarily **defensive and reconnaissance-oriented.** Operating near the vital Panama Canal, *S-26* contributed to the early efforts to secure this critical waterway against potential Axis threats. Its mission was part of the initial wartime deployment of US naval assets to establish a defensive posture. The patrol's lack of confirmed enemy contact and its cautious approach to an unidentified merchant ship indicate that **commerce interdiction** was not its immediate, aggressive objective in this specific area. Instead, it was likely tasked with maintaining vigilance and reporting any suspicious activity.

**Notable Successes or Failures:** The *S-26* had no combat successes during its brief war patrol. Its significant "failure" was its tragic loss due to a collision with *USS S-44* on January 24, 1942, shortly after completing its first war patrol. This event, occurring just off the Panama Canal, was a devastating blow, resulting in the loss of 46 lives (43 men and 3 officers) and a valuable submarine asset at a critical time for the US Navy. The extensive search and salvage operations that followed, involving multiple ships and divers, highlight the immediate and significant impact of this loss.

**Impact on Enemy Logistics or Operations:** The *S-26*'s patrols had no direct impact on enemy logistics or operations, as it did not engage or sink any enemy vessels. Its loss, however, represented a reduction in the US submarine force, albeit by an older vessel, at a moment when every asset was vital for the war effort.

## Long-term Impact & Lessons Learned

**Evolution of Submarine Warfare:** The loss of *USS S-26* due to a collision, coupled with the early combat experiences of other *S-boats*, underscored the urgent need for more advanced submarines. The *S-class* boats were quickly recognized as inadequate for the demands of long-range, offensive warfare in the vast Pacific. This accelerated the production and deployment of the superior *Gato* and *Balao* class fleet submarines, which became the true workhorses of the US submarine force in the Pacific. The incident also highlighted the critical importance of improved navigation, communication protocols, and formation keeping, especially during nighttime operations in wartime conditions, lessons that were continuously refined throughout the conflict.

**Lessons that Influenced Post-War Submarine Design or Tactics:**

- **Improved Safety and Navigation:** The collision directly emphasized the need for better navigation aids, communication systems, and training to prevent friendly fire incidents, a lesson that resonated through all naval operations. Post-war designs prioritized more advanced sensors and control systems.

- **Crew Comfort and Endurance:** The mention of air conditioning's benefit in tropical waters (from the *S-44* report) foreshadowed the increasing focus on habitability and environmental control in submarine design, crucial for maintaining crew effectiveness during extended patrols.

- **Salvage and Rescue:** The extensive, albeit ultimately unsuccessful, salvage efforts demonstrated the challenges and limitations of deep-water rescue and recovery. This experience influenced the development of specialized submarine rescue vehicles and techniques in the post-war era.

**Relevance to Modern Submarine Operations:** The fundamental challenges faced by *S-26* – maintaining vigilance, managing crew endurance, and navigating safely in company – remain relevant. Modern submarines, despite their technological sophistication, still operate in a challenging environment where precise navigation, clear communication, and robust safety protocols are paramount to prevent accidents and ensure mission success. The human element, including crew morale and training, continues to be a cornerstone of effective submarine operations.

**This Crew's Legacy in Naval History:** The crew of *USS S-26* represents the initial wave of American submariners who answered the call to duty at the very beginning of World War II. Their patrols, though uneventful in terms of combat, were part of the vital, immediate response to the Pearl Harbor attack, defending critical US assets. Their tragic loss, not in battle but through an operational accident, serves as a poignant reminder of the inherent dangers and sacrifices associated with submarine service, regardless of direct enemy engagement. They are part of the broader legacy of American naval personnel who served with dedication during a pivotal moment in history.

# Glossary of Naval Terms

## A

**Aft Torpedo Room:** The compartment at the stern (rear) of a submarine where stern torpedo tubes are located and torpedoes are stored and maintained.

**Ascent:** The process of a submerged submarine rising to the surface.

**Astern:** A command to apply reverse power to the propellers, causing the vessel to move backward or slow its forward motion.

## B

**Battle Stations:** A state of maximum readiness for combat, where all crew members are at their assigned posts to operate weapons, control damage, and maneuver the submarine.

**Bow Tubes:** The torpedo tubes located at the bow (front) of the submarine, used for firing torpedoes at targets ahead of the vessel.

**Bridge:** The open-air platform on top of the conning tower or sail, used for navigation and observation when the submarine is on the surface.

**Buoyancy:** The upward force exerted by water that opposes the weight of an immersed object. Submarines control their buoyancy using ballast tanks to submerge or surface.

## C

**Circular Run:** A dangerous torpedo malfunction where the torpedo fails to follow its set course and instead turns in a circle, potentially returning to strike the submarine that fired it.

**Conning Tower:** A small, pressure-proof compartment located above the main hull of a submarine, from which the commanding officer directs the vessel, especially during attacks.

**Convoy:** A group of merchant ships or troop transports traveling together, typically protected by a screen of naval escort vessels.

## D

**Down the Throat (shot):** A high-risk torpedo attack aimed directly at the bow of an approaching enemy vessel, requiring precise timing and calculation.

## E

**Electric Torpedo:** A type of torpedo, such as the Mark 18, propelled by an electric motor. Its primary advantage was that it did not leave a visible wake, making it harder for targets to detect and evade.

**End Around:** A tactic where a submarine surfaces and uses its superior surface speed to race ahead of a target's path to get into a favorable attack position.

**Escape Lung:** A breathing apparatus (e.g., Momsen Lung) designed to allow crew members to escape from a sunken submarine by providing a supply of oxygen for the ascent.

**Escape Trunk:** A small, floodable compartment or airlock used by the crew to exit a sunken submarine.

**Escorts:** Warships, such as destroyers or frigates, tasked with protecting a convoy or fleet from submarine and air attacks.

## F

**Fantail:** The rearmost, overhanging part of a ship's stern. On a submarine, it is the area above the stern torpedo tubes.

**Fish:** A common slang term for a torpedo.

**Forward Torpedo Room:** The compartment at the bow (front) of a submarine where the bow torpedo tubes are located and torpedoes are stored, loaded, and maintained.

**Frigate:** A type of warship, larger than a corvette but smaller than a destroyer, often used for escort and anti-submarine duties.

## I

**Intercept:** The action of maneuvering a submarine to cross the path of a reported enemy vessel or convoy for the purpose of an attack.

## J

**JANAC:** Acronym for the Joint Army-Navy Assessment Committee, a U.S. body established during World War II to analyze and verify claims of enemy ships sunk by U.S. forces.

## K

**Knots:** A unit of speed equal to one nautical mile per hour (approximately 1.15 mph), used to measure the speed of ships and submarines.

## M

**Mark 14 Torpedo:** The standard U.S. Navy submarine-launched steam-powered torpedo during World War II. It was known for early reliability issues but was powerful, leaving a visible wake.

**Mark 18 Torpedo:** A U.S. Navy electric torpedo developed during World War II. It was slower than the Mark 14 but was highly valued for being wakeless, making it ideal for stealthy attacks.

**Medal of Honor:** The highest and most prestigious military decoration awarded by the United States government for acts of valor.

## N

**Night Surface Attack:** A tactic where a submarine attacks on the surface under the cover of darkness, allowing for higher speeds and the use of radar to find targets.

## O

**Operate Independently:** To conduct a war patrol without being part of a coordinated group (wolf-pack), giving the submarine commander more freedom of action.

## P

**P-boat:** A designation for a patrol boat, typically a small vessel used for coastal patrol and anti-submarine warfare.

**Patrol Area:** A specific, designated sector of the ocean where a submarine is assigned to conduct its patrol.

**Patrol:** The primary operational mission of a submarine, involving a tour of duty in a designated area of the ocean to search for and attack enemy shipping.

**Periscope:** An optical instrument with lenses and prisms that allows a submerged submarine to view the surface of the water.

**POW:** Acronym for Prisoner of War, a person captured and held by an enemy power during a conflict.

**PPI:** Acronym for Plan Position Indicator, the circular display screen of a radar system that shows a map-like view of the surrounding area.

## R

**Radar:** A detection system that uses radio waves to determine the range, angle, or velocity of objects, critical for detecting ships at night or in poor visibility.

## S

**SS:** The U.S. Navy hull classification symbol for a diesel-electric attack submarine.

**Stern Tubes:** The torpedo tubes located at the stern (rear) of the submarine, allowing it to fire torpedoes at targets behind it.

**Submerged:** The state of a submarine operating completely underwater.

**Surface Attack:** An attack conducted while the submarine is on the surface, as opposed to a submerged attack using the periscope.

**Surfaced:** The state of a submarine operating on the surface of the water.

## T

**TBT:** Acronym for Target Bearing Transmitter, an optical sighting device used on the surface to take visual bearings of a target for torpedo attacks.

**TDC:** Acronym for Torpedo Data Computer, an analog computer that calculated the firing solution for a torpedo attack by integrating submarine and target data.

**Torpedo Run:** The final phase of an attack, during which the submarine maneuvers into the correct position to fire its torpedoes at the target.

## W

**Wolf-pack:** A tactic where multiple submarines coordinate their attacks against a single convoy to overwhelm its defenses.

# Most Important Passages

## First Enemy Contact and Attack Decision

> *Wednesday, August 13: At 1224 while on submerged patrol, sighted U.S.S. NEW YORK, hull number BB-34, on southerly course. Sent beam in eastern part of patrol area. Decided to attack. Bearing high speed range was never closed to less than 8700 yards. Six minutes after sighting NEW YORK, one destroyer was sighted. Twelve minutes later made out second destroyer. Forty minutes after first group passed cut of area and NEW YORK was observed to be zigzagging. Attack abandoned. It had been assumed that any target group passing through area would pass within 2 to 3 miles of submarine as seen 5 to 6 miles lateral miles long in an east and west direction, hence, the first day's patrol had been made on east and west courses, but when the U.S.S. NEW YORK was sighted and was passing through the center of the area on the short axis of the ellipse, the S-26 was on the eastern edge of the area on a north and south track. Subsequent patrolling and balancing was conducted in the center of the area. (p. 10)*

**Significance:** This passage demonstrates early tactical decision-making during training exercises, showing how the submarine commander learned to position the vessel for optimal attack opportunities and the challenges of closing range on fast-moving targets with escorts.

## Destroyer Encounter During Patrol

> *Friday, August 15: While patrolling submerged on westerly course sighted destroyer dead ahead on westerly course distant 9000 yards. Began approach. Destroyer, a four piper, proved to be an old destroyer distant 9000 yards. Began approach. Destroyer, a four piper, proved to be an old destroyer. Fired by sound, 600 yards from track, high parallax, 900 starboard track. Estimated course 250°, estimated speed 12 knots. (p. 10)*

**Significance:** This passage illustrates the submarine's combat approach methodology, including the use of sound-based firing solutions and the technical challenges of calculating firing angles and target movement during submerged operations.

## Daily Provisions and Ration Cost

> *0000-2400, August 15th Bread 30 lbs. Vienna Sausage 15 lbs. Sausage 8 lbs. Beets, and 4 lbs. Potatoes 28 lbs. Pork loin 24 lbs. Tomatoes, and 14 lbs. Corn starch 10 lbs. Cocoa 1 lb. Milk 7 lbs. Beans 5 lbs. Bologna 7 lbs. Onions 30 lbs. Tomatoes 9 lbs. Sausage, liver 6 lbs. Butter 7 lbs.*
>
> *The daily average cost of ration was 0.9699. (p. 19)*

**Significance:** This detailed provisioning record provides insight into the daily life and logistics of submarine operations, showing the variety and quantity of food needed to sustain the crew and the careful cost accounting maintained even during wartime operations.

## Rescue Operations with USS Mallard

> *U.S.S. MALLARD - Sunday, January 25, 1942. 1600 Commenced 3 and party reported on board, ships maneuvering on various courses and speeds continuing search. The ship then plowed through magnetic bands using the bow surf rider marker buoy to identify with magnetic bands and the bow surf rider marker buoy to identify with magnetic bands and the bow surf buoyed spot. 2105 Ceased magnetic sweeping. Sent boats to drag instead for objects, by grapnel so that sensitive mine might be used. 2115 USS SANDPIPER busy apparently stopped watching, whaleboats and USS SANDPIPER boats working together to develope contacts. 2230 MALLARD small boat drag hooked heavy strain. 2235 USS SANDPIPER pinging and sensitive mike working - No Answers. 2256 Ahead aid speed, course 045 mag. 2302 Stopped, lying to - Ships heading 85 mag. 2340 Ahead 1/3. (p. 38)*

**Significance:** This passage documents a critical search and rescue operation, showing the coordinated efforts of multiple vessels using various detection methods including magnetic sweeping and dragging operations, likely searching for a sunken submarine or wreckage.

## Diving Emergency and Communication Breakdown

> *1800 NOON complete. The ship then plowed through magnetic bands using the bow surf rider marker buoy to identify with magnetic bands and the bow surf buoyed spot. Jan 28, 1942. Diver surfaced 3 sudden gusty winds. 1st Diver - DENISTON, H.D. GMic. 1820 Diver dressed - phones OK. 1823 Diver going down. 1825 At 100 feet, Diver OK. 1826 At 200 feet, Diver OK. 1827 At 250 feet, XXXXXXXX.From diver: Something fouled on my hose. 1827-30 From diver: Take me Up. 1829 Taking diver up to 100 feet. 1830-30 From diver: OK - hold that - stand off - hold that - stand off, I have turn under stage. 1831-30 From diver: take me up a little. 1832 From the diver: ON the stage. 1832k-30 To diver: What are you doing? A: I feel OK - my arms are tired. To diver: We a re going to lower stage 10 1833k45 From diver: hold stage. 1834k-30 Started time. 1836 To diver: Was wire fouled around descending line? A: Yes on descending line. (p. 48)*

**Significance:** This dramatic passage captures a dangerous diving operation with real-time communications between the diver and surface crew, showing the hazards of deep-water salvage work and the critical importance of clear communication during emergencies.

## Securing New Descending Line

> *1251 Preparing diver to go over.(FRADLER, H.H. SF1c.). Purpose of this dive is to secure new descending line to gun. 1544 Over the side - going down. 1549 On*

*the submarine. 1551 From diver: Take me up. 1555 On the stage. XXXXXX.120 ft. 1603 Diver coming up to 80. 1606 Diver coming up to 70. 1610 Diver coming up to 60. 1621 Diver coming up to 50. 1625 Diver on deck - to the chamber. 1635 Preparing diver to go over the side.(SNODDEN, O.T.T. Elec.,) The purpose of this dive was to secure descending line to the gun. 1654 Over the side - going down. 1700 On the bottom. 1710 Left the bottom. 1713 Diver coming up - 120 ft. 1721 " " " - 90 ft. 1729 " " " - 80 ft. 1733 " " " - 70 ft. 1743 " " " - 60 ft. 1754 " " " - 50 ft. 1757 Diver on deck - to chamber. (p. 57)*

**Significance:** This passage documents the meticulous and time-consuming process of deep-sea diving operations on a sunken submarine, showing the careful depth management and decompression procedures required for diver safety during salvage operations.

## Diver's Personal Account of Salvage Attempt

*STATEMENT OF GRIFFIN, J.D. CMic. (Dive 1). Upon reaching the bottom I found the starboard seat of the gun to which the descending line was secured to be carried away. I landed outboard of the submarine, pulled myself up on deck, and proceeded to resecure the descending line, paying particular attention that it was clear of all obstacles that might foul in the way of future dives. I secured the descending line to the starboard life line stanchion abreast of the conning tower. I cleared the blow nose as well as I could and then went aft on starboard fairwater to find the air salvage connection. I found it alright but had difficulty trying to loosen the fitting as I could not get a good purchase on wrench. My left arm was very tired from heaving on the blow nose and descending line. So I though it best to start back to my descending line before tiring too much. I could say that visibility is about 12 feet. The submarine is on an even keel as near as I could judge. One section of the life line on the starboard side just forward of fairwater is carried away. (p. 66)*

**Significance:** This first-person account from a Navy diver provides rare human perspective on the dangerous and exhausting work of attempting to salvage a sunken submarine, including specific technical details about the vessel's condition and the physical challenges faced underwater.

## Summary of Events and Crew Morale Assessment

*Feb 7(Contd). 1216 - Ahead on both engines proceeding to Balboa in accordance with instructions. 1840 - Off station ship, pilot came on board. 1847 - Moored starboard side to USS GOLDSBOROUGH at Pier 18 So. Pilot left the ship. Feb 8. 0758 - Underway. 0802 - Transit completed, pilot left the ship off Cristobal 1628 - Moored starboard side to North side Pier 1, Submarine Base, Coco Solo, C.Z. 9. Torpedoes were kept in the ready condition at all times. No torpedoes were fired that had excessive loss of air. 10. The general weather conditions during the two weeks off the MALLARD in the Canal Zone of Panama were ideal. A strong current was experienced at irregular times, which made station keeping off the MALLARD difficult. 11. The ship was quite habitable although the temperature of the after battery heated up because the engines were not run continually. 12. The morale of the crew was good. They were kept busy by daily ship drills and school of the ship. During week day mornings gunnery exercises were held about two miles South of the Pier and all new seaman and fireman received instruction in pointing and training, all men fired the pistol within the past year received instruction and fired several clips of ammunition. Semaphore and blinker drills were held on a deck every day. (p. 85)*

**Significance:** This summary passage provides comprehensive insight into the operational readiness, living conditions, and crew training regimen during the patrol, demonstrating the Navy's emphasis on maintaining combat readiness and morale even during non-combat operations.

## War Patrol Mission Orders

*This vessel conducted a war patrol as directed by Commander Submarines, Off-shore Patrol, Pacific, Mallard BOARD of January, 1942. On January 24, 1942, departed Coco Solo, Canal Zone on January 24, 1942, transited Canal and anchored in Balboa Harbor. On January 25, 1942, got underway and proceeded to assigned patrol area. On January 26, 1942, arrived in patrol area and began patrol. Kept in column on starboard quarter until 2100 when took station ahead. Distance between vessels was 1000 yards. Patrolled in assigned area until January 31, 1942, when ordered to return to Balboa. At 2000, reached Point 85, about 6 miles off shore and 20 miles from Balboa. Proceeded on surface toward Balboa. At 2045, sighted lights and changed course. At 2100, sighted lights and changed course. At 2130, sighted lights and changed course. At 2200, sighted lights and changed course. Arrived at Balboa at 2300. At 2330, anchored in Balboa Harbor. On February 1, 1942, got underway and proceeded to Coco Solo. Arrived at Coco Solo at 1100. Moored alongside USS GOLDSBOROUGH. On February 2, 1942, got underway and proceeded to Balboa. Arrived at Balboa at 1600. Anchored in Balboa Harbor. On February 3, 1942, got underway and proceeded to Coco Solo. Arrived at Coco Solo at 1100. Moored alongside USS GOLDSBOROUGH. (p. 95)*

**Significance:** This passage documents the submarine's first war patrol mission during the critical early months of WWII, showing the transition from training to actual combat operations and the careful navigation required in potentially hostile waters near the Panama Canal.

## Press Representatives Inspection Visit

*The following representatives of the press accompanied Admiral Salter on inspection trip to the scene of salvage operations:*

*Mr. Richard Armstrong International News Service Mr. Brodie Burnham Panama American. (p. 104)*

**Significance:** This brief passage reveals the public relations aspect of naval operations, showing that even during wartime salvage operations, the Navy coordinated with press representatives to document and report on significant events, indicating the importance of the S-26 incident.

# War Patrol Reports

# START OF REEL

# JOB NO. H-108

AR-315-76

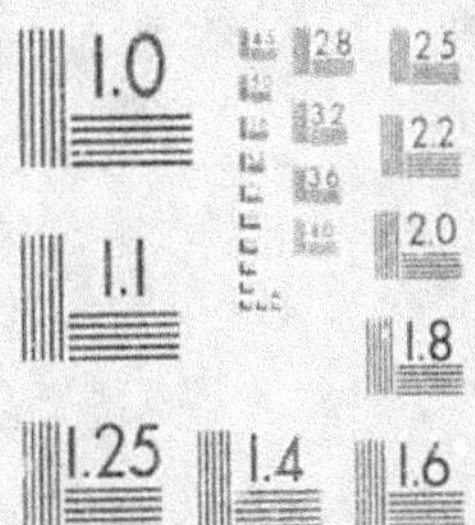


OPERATOR CGM

DATE 8/21/78

# THIS MICROFILM IS THE PROPERTY OF THE UNITED STATES GOVERNMENT

MICROFILMED BY
NPPSO—NAVAL DISTRICT WASHINGTON
MICROFILM SECTION

REEL TARGET - START AND END
NDW-NPPSO-5210/1 (6-78)

ALL MATERIAL
ON THIS REEL
IS
DECLASSIFIED

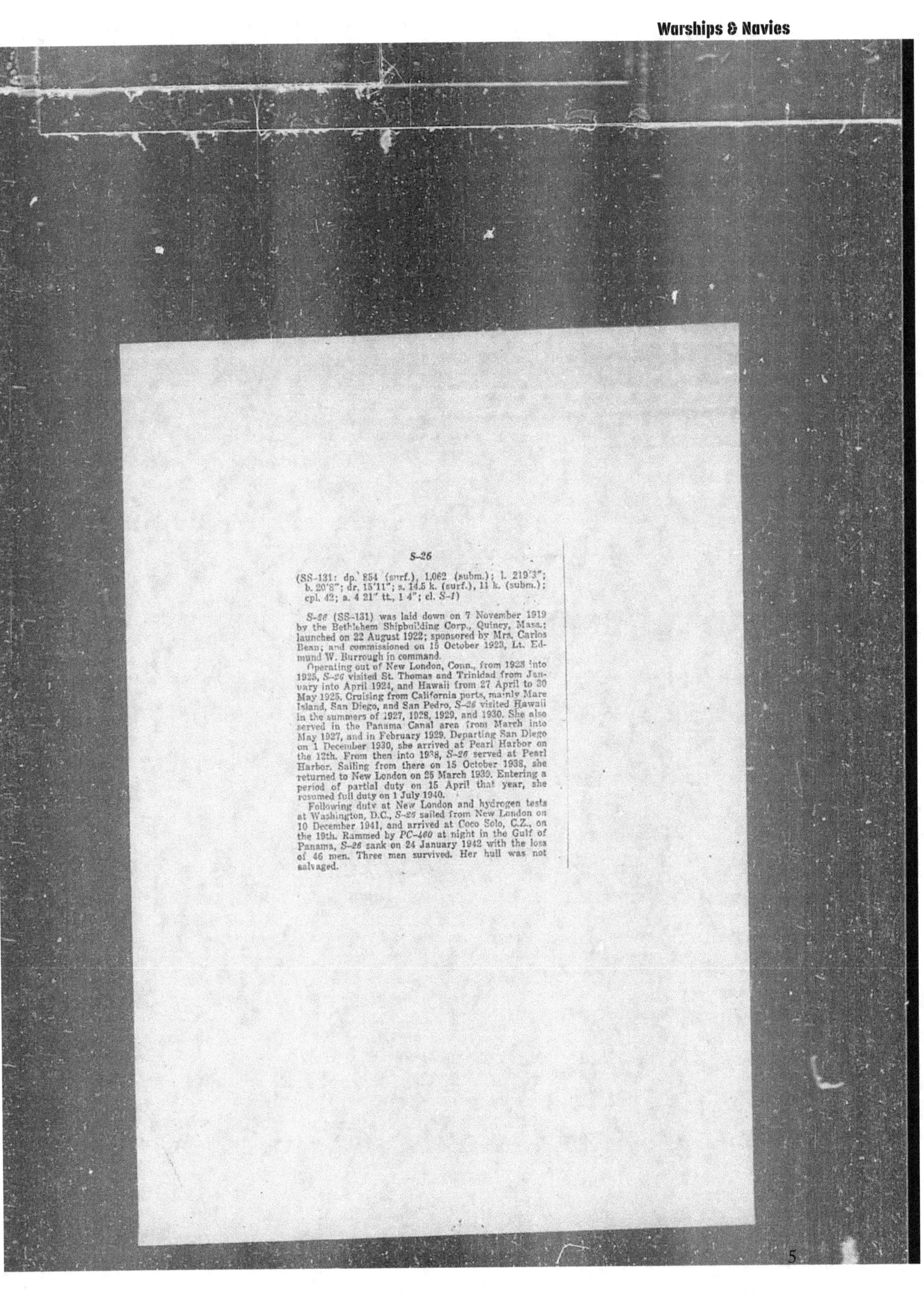

### *S-26*

(SS-131: dp. 854 (surf.), 1,062 (subm.); l. 219'3"; b. 20'8"; dr. 15'11"; s. 14.5 k. (surf.), 11 k. (subm.); cpl. 42; a. 4 21" tt., 1 4"; cl. *S-1*)

*S-26* (SS-131) was laid down on 7 November 1919 by the Bethlehem Shipbuilding Corp., Quincy, Mass.; launched on 22 August 1922; sponsored by Mrs. Carlos Bean; and commissioned on 15 October 1923, Lt. Edmund W. Burrough in command.

Operating out of New London, Conn., from 1923 into 1925, *S-26* visited St. Thomas and Trinidad from January into April 1924, and Hawaii from 27 April to 30 May 1925. Cruising from California ports, mainly Mare Island, San Diego, and San Pedro, *S-26* visited Hawaii in the summers of 1927, 1928, 1929, and 1930. She also served in the Panama Canal area from March into May 1927, and in February 1929. Departing San Diego on 1 December 1930, she arrived at Pearl Harbor on the 12th. From then into 1938, *S-26* served at Pearl Harbor. Sailing from there on 15 October 1938, she returned to New London on 25 March 1939. Entering a period of partial duty on 15 April that year, she resumed full duty on 1 July 1940.

Following duty at New London and hydrogen tests at Washington, D.C., *S-26* sailed from New London on 10 December 1941, and arrived at Coco Solo, C.Z., on the 19th. Rammed by *PC-460* at night in the Gulf of Panama, *S-26* sank on 24 January 1942 with the loss of 46 men. Three men survived. Her hull was not salvaged.

SS131/A16

SUBMARINE DIVISION FIFTY-ONE
U.S.S. S-26

C/o Postmaster, New York, N.Y.
Morgan Annex, Navy Desk
August 18, 1941



From: The Commanding Officer.
To: The Commander Submarine Squadron FIVE.

Subject: Patrol Run - Report on.

Reference: (a) CSS-5 conf. serial 0153 of August 6, 1941, Annex C.

Enclosure: (A) Patrol Diary.
(B) Summary of Required Data.

1. The S-26 conducted a six-day war patrol beginning 0500 from Provincetown Anchorage August 12, 1941, and ending 0900 in patrol area off Cape Ann August 17, 1941. The following report and comments are submitted herewith.

2. The first, fifth and sixth days were surface patrol and the second, third and fourth days submerged patrol. The patrol area was off Cape Ann. During the days of surface patrol the following number of dives were made to avoid detection:

| DATE | TIME OF DIVE | CHARACTER OF TARGET |
|---|---|---|
| Tuesday, Aug. 12 | 81" | Merchant steamer. |
| Saturday, Aug. 16 | 75" | Three planes. |
| Saturday, Aug. 16 | 65" | U.S.S. NEW YORK. |

Numerous small fishing boats were present throughout the area, lying to fishing or passing through, apparently operating out of Gloucester.



3. SURFACE PATROL

On surface patrol in the daytime, ship was rigged for dive, bow planes rigged in, riding the vents, one section on watch, steering in control room. Bridge personnel consisted of O.O.D., quartermaster, two regular day lookouts and any additional volunteer lookouts, generally about two. Day lookouts were men from the relief section. They stood two-hour watches. At night, ship was in same condition except battery ventilation was shifted to the engineroom during the battery charge. The helmsman steered from the conning tower and wore battle telephones in communication with the torpedo room. The Mk XIV director was mounted on the bridge. Torpedo firing circuit was cut in to the conning tower and kept energized. Torpedo tube shutters were open, outer doors closed, impulse pressure built

- 1 -

SS131/A16 SUBMARINE DIVISION FIFTY-ONE
U.S.S. S-26

August 18, 1941

CONFIDENTIAL DECLASSIFIED

Subject: Patrol Run - Report on.

- - - - - - - - - - - - - - - - - - - - - - - - - - - - - - - -

up in tanks, and pressure built up in forward trim tank. At night three battle lookouts were on watch. They stood no other duties. They stood one-hour watches, reliefs being staggered every twenty minutes. System worked very well. Binoculars for the lookouts were inadequate and insufficient.

No night attacks were made. It is not known whether any targets ever passed through the area or not. None were sighted but on several nights a darkened target could have passed within 500 yards and would never have been sighted due to poor visibility conditions.

4. SUBMERGED PATROL

Submerged patrol from 0600 to 1800 was conducted for three days. On the first day patrol was extended nearly to the eastern limit of the area. Shortly after noon on this day the New York with screening destroyers was sighted about eight miles to the westward. An approach was started but range could not be closed to more than 8700 yards. The target group apparently ran through the center of area on a southerly course and caught the S-26 in the eastern end of the area, unable to get in an attack. As the area is eighteen miles long in an east and west direction and only eight miles wide in a north and south direction it was assumed that any target group would pass through the area along the long axis rather than the short axis. This assumption proved to be erroneous and the second and third day's patrol was confined to the center of the area in order to be in position to get in an attack. No other regular targets were sighted, however.

Conditions submerged were very comfortable except for excessive sweating of the boat. Condensation dripped from the frames and sides. The decks were wet and clothing and bedding at the end of three days were very damp. The temperature never exceeded 87° and the relative humidity was comparatively low, averaging about 66°. It was noted that during balancing at deep depths the relative humidity dropped off 4 to 5% as did the temperature. No cooking was done submerged.

- 2 -

SS131/A16 SUBMARINE DIVISION FIFTY-ONE
U.S.S. S-26

August 18, 1941

CONFIDENTIAL

Subject: Patrol Run - Report on.

- - - - - - - - - - - - - - - - - - - - - - - - - - - - - - - -

The smoking lamp was lighted for ten minutes each hour submerged.

No air purification was resorted to. The percent CO2 at the end of the all-day dives was about 1.5%.

The hydrogen concentration in the boat was not taken as the portable hydrogen detector is at the factory for repair. Highest percent as recorded on the installed detectors was 0.1%.

The increase in air pressure in the boat was exceedingly low, averaging only about one inch after 12 hours. It was not necessary to run the compressors or vent the boat to reduce the pressure.

5. BALANCING

Balancing, with stop trim, was conducted during the three-day submerged patrol for a total of 14.95 hours. This included periods of continuous stop trim balancing of 2.1, 3.1, 3.5, and 3.6 hours. Had it not been for the fact that noon position reports had to be made, balancing could have been continued for much longer periods. Balancing at periscope depth was found to be impossible even in smooth water. The best level was found to be at 80-100 feet with the boat oscillating between 70 and 110 feet.

Balancing at deeper depths, 120-130 feet, required much more pumping of water and usually if the boat started down, the trim pump was unable to pump fast enough to stop the descent. On two occasions the boat was taken to 193 feet, once by running down on the motors and the second time by drifting down during balancing. Only a couple of minor leaks were found at this depth. During the balancing the crew moved about the boat freely and bilges were pumped but no difficulty was experienced in maintaining the stop trim.

- 3 -

SS131/A16 SUBMARINE DIVISION FIFTY-ONE
U.S.S. S-26

CONFIDENTIAL August 18, 1941

Subject: Patrol Run - Report on.

- - - - - - - - - - - - - - - - - - - - - - - - - - - - - - - -

6. MEALS AND PROVISIONS

During the three-day submerged patrol, the inverted order of meals was tried out. Meal hours were:

1900 - Breakfast.

2400 - Dinner.

0500 - Supper.

Patrol reports of other boats have claimed the following advantages for this inverted order of meals.

(a) No cooking is done submerged and there are no cooking odors in the boat.

(b) The heat from the range is eliminated while submerged.

(c) The men are able to sleep all day and be up and about at night on the surface.

In answer to these claims it may be said that there are numerous foods which may be cooked without obnoxious odors; practically everything except fried foods, cabbage, turnips and sauerkraut.

Likewise the heat given off by the range may be undesirable in the tropics but even during this patrol with the injection temperature at 62° the heat from the range would have been desirable. Both the odor and heat situation could easily be taken care of by new boats with air conditioning.

- 4 -

SS131/A16 SUBMARINE DIVISION FIFTY-ONE
U.S.S. S-26

CONFIDENTIAL August 18, 1941

Subject: Patrol Run - report of.

- - - - - - - - - - - - - - - - - - - - - - - - - - - - - - - -

As for the men sleeping all day and being up all night, such was not actually found to be true. The men slept both night and day except when on watch and when dinner was served at midnight only half the food was eaten. During the daytime while submerged, about three times as many sandwiches were eaten as is ordinarily done during the night.

In general the experiment was a failure. All hands were unanimous in the opinion that the idea is fine theoretically, but not practical. Actually, it does not accomplish the desired purpose, that of keeping all hands up and about all night.

From a disadvantageous viewpoint, it requires all meals to be eaten on the surface. This may mean eating three meals in seven or eight hours on patrols during periods of long daylight. This is not enough time between meals. In rough weather, eating on the surface generally, of necessity, consists of sandwiches and soup because very little cooking can be done and mess tables cannot be set up. Hence, it would be much better to eat submerged where it is calm, even if the meals were mainly of the cold variety. From a psychological standpoint, it is not believed possible to ask a man to eat sauerkraut and frankfurters at 0500 and expect him to turn to on them with a hearty appetite when he knows full well that it really is breakfast time even though the commanding officer says it is supper time.

In summing up, it is firmly believed that the normal meals should be served at the normal times and cooking submerged is feasible and will not entail too much discomfort from heat or odors.

"Nescafe", a special pulverized coffee, requiring only the addition of hot water to make coffee,was experimented with. It is a fair substitute but can instantly be detected from real coffee. The hotter the water, the more like coffee it tastes but as it cools, a distinct malt taste becomes noticeable. In general, it was not popular. Everyone preferred the regular coffee to "Nescafe".

- 5 -

SS131/A16 SUBMARINE DIVISION FIFTY-ONE
U.S.S. S-26

CONFIDENTIAL August 18, 1941

Subject: Patrol Run - report of.

- - - - - - - - - - - - - - - - - - - - - - - - - - - - -

7. MORALE

The morale of the crew was excellent. To many, it was a new experience being submerged all day. Reading seemed to be the most popular. Some acey ducey was played but not more than under normal conditions.

8. COMMUNICATIONS

Noon position reports were sent by periscope antenna; communication was fair. The signal strength of the tender was very low, so low that it was necessary to shut down the transmitter in order to hear the receipt for the transmitted message.

9. SOUND

Sound conditions in Area 5 were only fair. The maximum range being 3000 to 4000 yards. This condition was observed on three different types of ships, a merchant steamer, an old type destroyer and the NEW YORK.

10. WEATHER, CURRENT

In general the weather was good with southerly winds prevailing, seas moderately rough and visibility conditions fair except on Saturday the 16th fog and passing showers prevailed with the visibility varying from one to four miles. Little or no current set was experienced in Area 5.

11. CHARGING

The battery was kept fully charged by charging with one engine during the night. Charging time averaged about eight hours each night.

- 6 -

SS131/A16 SUBMARINE DIVISION FIFTY-ONE
U.S.S. S-26

CONFIDENTIAL

August 18, 1941

Subject: Patrol Run - report on.

- - - - - - - - - - - - - - - - - - - - - - - - - - - - - - - -

12. WATER

The evaporator was operated an average of about nine hours each night. Only the exhaust of one engine running at 2/3 speed was utilized. Sufficient water was made to refill the fresh water tank nightly. Water consumption averaged about 3.6 gallons per man per day.

13. APPROACHES MADE

Wednesday, August 13: At 1224 while on submerged patrol, sighted U.S.S. NEW YORK, hull down, range 16000 yards, on southerly course. S-26 then in eastern part of area. Approach was started but even by using high speed range was never closed to less than 8700 yards. Six minutes after sighting NEW YORK, mast of one destroyer screen sighted. Twelve minutes later mast of far destroyer screen was sighted. At 1309 target group passed out of area and NEW YORK was observed to be picking up plane. Attack abandoned. It had been assumed that any target group passing through area would pass through along the long axis inasmuch as area 5 is eighteen miles long in an east and west direction and only eight miles wide in a north and south direction, hence, the first day's submerged patrol had been made on east and west courses, but when the U.S.S. NEW YORK was sighted she was passing through the center of the area on the short axis and the S-26 was caught way out of position to get in an attack. Subsequent patrolling and balancing was conducted in the center of the area.

Friday, August 15: While patrolling submerged on westerly course sighted destroyer dead ahead on westerly course distant 9000 yards. Began approach. Destroyer, not flying baker, proved to be an old type. At 3000-yard range went to 80 feet to prevent detection and simulated firing by sound, 600 yards from track, high parallax, 90° starboard track. Estimated course 250°, estimated speed 12 knots.

- 7 -

SS131/A16 SUBMARINE DIVISION FIFTY-ONE
U.S.S. S-26

August 18, 1941

DECLASSIFIED CONFIDENTIAL

Subject: Patrol Run - report on.

- - - - - - - - - - - - - - - - - - - - - - - - - - - - - - - - - - -

Saturday, August 16: An hour after surfacing after having been forced to dive by three planes, the U.S.S. NEW YORK was sighted dead ahead at 1504 on southerly course, 30 degree port angle on bow, distant 6000 yards. Dove and closed at high speed for attack, firing straight bow shots, 105 port track angle, 2200-yard range. Visibility was very poor due to fog. Estimated enemy course 210°, estimated speed 15 knots.

MISCELLANEOUS:

At about 0940 on Saturday, August 16, a patrol gunboat, later identified as the P57 appeared out of the mist about three miles distant and challenged the S-26 with "AA". S-26 answered, exchanging calls. Gunboat then challenged with the two letters EP several times. This did not fit any of the current recognition signals which are all three letters. It was realized that she was using a system which has been in a reserve on board status since June. This was broken out of the safe and proper reply sent. By this time both ships had closed to about half mile range. In subsequent exchange of messages by semaphore it was learned that gunboat had not been informed that the system he was using, CSP 1023) has been in reserve status since June. He apparently did not have the current recognition signals and furthermore he did not know that submarines were and will be operating in area off Cape Ann for the next two weeks.

14. This patrol was excellent training for both officers and men, especially the night battle lookouts. It was the first time real balancing with stop trim had been done for any length of time. For many of the crew it was their first all day dive. No injuries or sickness occurred. No materiel failures were experienced. The patrol was considered to be highly successful and instructive, with the exception that no opportunities for attacks at night targets were presented.

- 8 -

SS131/A16 SUBMARINE DIVISION FIFTY-ONE
U.S.S. S-26

August 18, 1941

DECLASSIFIED

Subject: Patrol Run - Report on.

- - - - - - - - - - - - - - - - - - - - - - - - - - - - - - - - -

However, this probably kept the night lookouts and O.O.D. more on the alert than if a target had come through after which there would probably have been a relaxation in vigilance. One recommendation is made, namely, that target groups passing through an area do so along the long axis of the area. This would decrease the possibility of the submerged submarine being caught so far from the track as to be unable to make an attack. Also, if balancing at deep depth she would probably detect the target with her sound gear.

E. C. Hawk
E. C. HAWK.

End

- 9 -

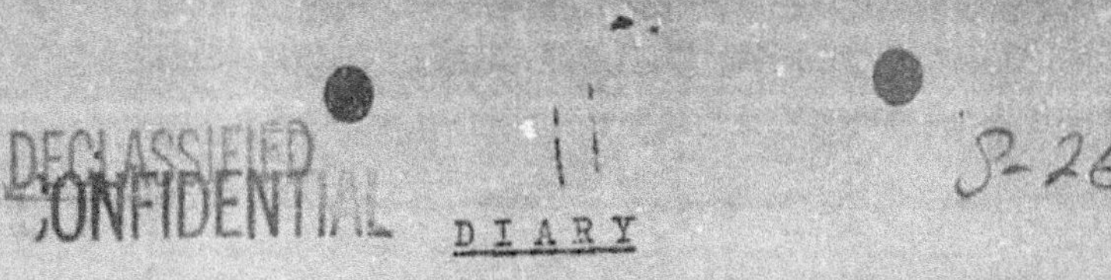

DECLASSIFIED
CONFIDENTIAL

S-26

DIARY

Tuesday, August 12: 0500 Underway from Provincetown for Patrol Area off Cape Ann. 0958 Made 1½ hour trim and balancing dive. Conducted surface patrol during the day on east and west courses. Submerged from 1306 until 1357 to avoid detection by small steamer passing through area on northerly course. During night patrolled on surface on north and south courses on line about 10 miles east of Cape Ann Light. Ship rigged for dive and night surprise fire. Charged battery, air banks and operated evaporator during night. No targets sighted.

Wednesday, August 13: 0545 Executed sunrise. 0653 Submerged for all day patrol. Dive delayed due to inability to clear 0600 position report to Commander Submarine Squadron Five. Patrolled on east and west courses at 2.6 knots. Sighted several small fishing boats during the day. At 1224 sighted U.S.S. NEW YORK, 8 miles to westward on a southerly course. Started approach. 1309 Abandoned attack; unable to get closer than 8700 yards. Resumed patrol at periscope depth. 1540 Went to 100 feet and conducted stop trim balancing until 1752. Came up to periscope depth, nothing in sight. 1800 Surfaced. Set course toward Cape Ann light. 1949 Executed sunset. Put ship in condition for night surprise attack. During the night patrolled on north and scuth courses on a line about 6 miles east of Cape Ann Light, at 2/3 speed on one engine. Charged batteries on other engine. Charged air banks, operated evaporators. No targets sighted during the night.

Thursday, August 14: 0546 Executed sunrise. 0558 Submerged for all day patrol on course 090° T. At 0730 went to 80 feet for stop trim balancing. 0840 Tried balancing at 120 foot depth. Found to be more difficult than at 80 feet. 0850 Ran down to 193 foot depth on motors. Two minor leaks noted, one around packing gland of steering control shaft through bridge deck, other leak in signal gun drain line union. 0900 Back to 120 foot level for more balancing. From 0900 until 1020 tried balancing at 120 foot level. Boat very sensitive, drifting down to 170, 180 and 193 foot depths, with trim pump not capable of pumping fast enough to arrest descent. 1020 Began balancing at 80 foot level. 1046 Sound reported hearing ship's screw on bearing 30° relative. Came to periscope depth on course 115° T. Sighted merchant steamer bearing 185° T distant two miles on course 250°. 1050 Changed course to 090° T and began patrolling at periscope depth. 1150 Changed course to 180°. Sighted small fishing boat bearing 250° T distant 2 miles. 1232 Changed course to 270° T. 1305 Heard two thuds which sounded like distant depth charges. Two similar thuds had previously been noted at 1115. May have been fishing boats using dynamite

- 1 -

ENCLOSURE "A"

DECLASSIFIED
CONFIDENTIAL DIARY(CONTINUED)

Thursday, August 14 (Cont'd): 1400 Changed course to 000° T. 1409 Went to 80 feet for balancing. 1739 Ceased balancing. Came to periscope depth, nothing in sight. 1800 Surfaced on course 270°. Went ahead 2/3 on both engines and swung ship for compass deviations. 1947 Executed sunset. Put ship in condition for night surprise attack. Began patrolling on north and south courses on line about 5 miles east of Cape Ann Light, at 2/3 speed on one engine. During the night charged battery on one engine, charged air banks and operated evaporator. No targets sighted during the night.

Friday, August 15: 0547 Executed sunrise. 0600 Submerged for all day patrol on course 090°. 0730 Sighted large steamer bearing 135° T on a westerly course, distant 5 miles. 0807 Went to 80 feet and began balancing with stop trim. Balanced for three hours, 9 minutes, depth varying from 70 to 115 feet. 1117 Went ahead on motors. Came up to periscope depth at 1140, nothing in sight. 1200 Sighted destroyer bearing 085° T distant 9000 yards, went to battle stations, started approach. 1215 Destroyer not flying baker, old 4-stack type. 1220 went to 80 feet at 3000 yard range to avoid detection. 1224 Simulated firing torpedoes by sound, 90° starboard track, 600 yards from track, high parallax, estimated enemy course 255° T, speed 12 knots. 1232 Came up to periscope depth. 1306 Changed course to 270° T. 1321 Sighted heavy cruiser bearing 240° T, distant 10000 yards on a southerly course. Went to battle stations, started approach. 1327 Cruiser identified as U.S.S. AUGUSTA. No baker flying. Her position about a mile south of area. Secured from battle stations, resumed patrol on course 270°. 1353 Went to 100 feet for balancing. Balanced from 1408 until 1747. 1747 Came to periscope depth, sighted small fishing boat 1½ miles astern. 1800 Surfaced on course 270°, went ahead 2/3 speed one engine. 1943 Executed sunset. Placed ship in condition for night surprise attack. During the night patrolled on north and south courses on a line about 5 miles east of Cape Ann Light, on one engine. Charged batteries with other engine. Charged air and operated evaporator. 2000 Sighted large passenger steamer bearing 230° T, distant 5 miles, headed east. 2230 Visibility reduced to 2 miles, passing showers set in.

Saturday, August 16: During mid-watch sounded fog signals from 0204 to 0230. 0548 Executed sunrise. Began surface patrol on course 000°. 0940 Exchanged calls and messages with Patrol Gunboat 57. 1025 Changed course to 180°. 1302 Sighted three planes coming in from east, distant 1 mile, altitude 500 feet. Made emergency dive to 80 feet. Time of dive 75 seconds. 1330 Came up to periscope depth, nothing in sight, visibility poor.

- 2 - ENCLOSURE "A"

CONFIDENTIAL DIARY ( CONTINUED)

Saturday, August 16 (Cont'd)

1408 Surfaced on course 000°, nothing in sight. Resumed surface patrol on one engine. 1504 Sighted U.S.S. NEW YORK dead ahead distant 3 miles, 30° port angle on bow. Dove (65") went to battle stations, began approach at high speed. 1521 Fired longitudinal spread of 4 torpedoes, 105 port track, zero gyro angles, 2200 yards from track. Estimated enemy course 210°, speed 15 knots, visibility very poor through periscope. 1536 Surfaced on course 000°, nothing in sight, visibility 2 miles. Resumed surface patrol on one engine on course 180°. 1942 Executed sunset. Placed ship in condition for night surprise attack. During night patrolled on north and south course, 4 miles east of Cape Ann Light, charged batteries on one engine, charged air banks, operated evaporator.

Sunday, August 17: 0549 Executed sunrise. Continued surface patrol until 0900. 0900 Proceeded to Provincetown, arriving 1300.

- 3 - ENCLOSURE "A"

S-26

CONFIDENTIAL

1. The data required by paragraph 6 of reference (a) is summarized below. All figures are from midnight to midnight with the exception of the entries regarding K.W.H. discharged submerged, auxiliary load on surface and K.W.H. charged. These figures are from 0600 to 0600. The reason for this being that the charging done during the night is covered completely and actually shows how many K.W.H. were put back into the battery following the all day dive.

| DATA REQUIRED | TUES 12th 0500-2400 | WED 13th 2400-2400 | THURS 14th 2400-2400 | FRI 15th 2400-2400 | SAT 16th 2400-2400 | SUN 17th 2400-0900 | AVERAGE FOR PATROL (5.4 DAYS) |
|---|---|---|---|---|---|---|---|
| (a) Amt potable water exp per man (5 officers, 43 men) (gals.) | 2.29 | 3.92 | 3.09 | 4.46 | 4.25 | 1.08 | 3.52 |
| (b) Amt battery water used (gals.) | | | | | | 303 | 50.5 |
| (c) Amt provisions exp | | | See separate list | | | | |
| (d) Amt potable water distilled (gals.) | 70 | 188 | 168 | 164 | 182 | 42 | 150 |
| (e) Fuel used (gals.) | 560 | 510 | 430 | 260 | 250 | 170 | 404 |
| (f) KWH disch, submerged | 579 | 1304 | 810 | 723 | 298 | | 687 |
| KWH aux load, surface | 576 | 347 | 363 | 272 | 577 | | 395 |
| KWH charged | 977 | 2219 | 1401 | 986 | 1146 | | 1246 |
| (g) Ave. high temp. | 75 | 87 | 84 | 83 | 69 | 68 | |
| Ave. low temp. | 64 | 78 | 81 | 81 | 66 | 64 | |
| % rel. humidity | 93 | 89 | 65 | 66 | 95 | 95 | |
| (h) Hours continuous balancing with stop trim. | .5 | 2.1 | 3.1<br>3.5 | 3.2<br>3.6 | - | - | |
| (i) Time taken on emergency quick dives | 58"<br>81" | 67" | 69" | 90" | 75"<br>65" | | |

ADDITIONAL DATA TAKEN

| | TUES | WED | THURS | FRI | SAT | SUN |
|---|---|---|---|---|---|---|
| Air pressure increase in boat at end of 12 hour dive | | .95" | .85" | 1.1" | | |
| %CO2 in boat at end of 12 hour dive | | 1.5 | 1.5 | 1.5 | | |
| Lube oil exp (gals.) | 20 | 80 | 20 | 20 | 20 | |
| Inject. temp, surface | 67 | 65 | 63 | 62 | 62 | 62 |

- 1 - ENCLOSURE "B"

DECLASSIFIED CONFIDENTIAL

| DATA | TUES 12th 0500- 2400 | WED 13th 2400- 2400 | THURS 14th 2400- 2400 | FRI 15th 2400- 2400 | SAT 16th 2400- 2400 | SUN 17th 2400- 0900 |
|---|---|---|---|---|---|---|
| Time of sunrise | 0545 | 0545 | 0546 | 0547 | 0548 | 0549 |
| Time of sunset | 1949 | 1947 | 1945 | 1943 | 1942 | 1941 |
| Time of moonrise (Last Quarter) | 2237 | 2309 | 2343 | 0030 | 0110 | |

ENCLOSURE "B"

- 2 -

(C) DAILY EXPENDITURE OF PROVISIONS

CONFIDENTIAL

0500-2400, Tuesday, August 12th

| | | | |
|---|---|---|---|
| Bread | 37 lbs | Eggs | 6 doz |
| Chipped beef | 6 lbs. | Cheese, Swiss | 2 lbs. |
| Coffee | 10 lbs. | Bacon | 5 lbs. |
| Sugar | 10 lbs. | Milk, evap. | 10 lbs. |
| Ham, tnd | 21 lbs. | Beef, Swiss(B&R) | 27 lbs. |
| Cabbage | 20 lbs. | Spinach, tnd | 7 lbs. |
| Turnips | 10 lbs. | Lettuce | 5 lbs. |
| Potatoes | 22 lbs. | Macaroni | 12½ lbs. |
| Butter | 7 lbs. | Tomatoes, tnd | 7 lbs. |
| Apples | 15 lbs. | Onions | 4 lbs. |
| | | Salami | 7 lbs. |
| | | Sausage, liver | 5 lbs. |

0000-2400, August 13th

| | | | |
|---|---|---|---|
| Pork & Beans | 7 lbs. | Coffee | 17 lbs. |
| Sugar | 17 lbs. | Lemons | 3 lbs. |
| Bread | 36 lbs. | Milk, evap | 10 lbs. |
| Butter | 6 lbs. | Bacon | 21 lbs. |
| Eggs | 5 doz. | Potatoes, sweet | 25 lbs. |
| Beef, Swiss, B&R | 25 lbs. | Potatoes | 9 lbs. |
| Asparagus, tnd | 7 lbs. | Spinach, tnd | 7 lbs. |
| Lettuce | 5 lbs. | Flour | 8 lbs. |
| Salami | 3 lbs. | Cheese, Swiss | 3 lbs. |
| Apples | 15 lbs. | Bologna | 3 lbs. |
| Onions | 4 lbs. | Sausage, liver | 5 lbs. |
| Lima beans, FF | 10 lbs. | Tomatoes, fresh | 5 lbs. |

0000-2400, August 14th

| | | | |
|---|---|---|---|
| Bread | 42 lbs. | Chicken | 16 lbs. |
| Butter | 6 lbs. | Corn, tnd | 7 lbs. |
| Flour | 12 lbs. | Coffee | 13 lbs. |
| Sugar | 15 lbs | Cheese, Swiss | 3 lbs. |
| Salami | 5 lbs. | Tomatoes | 5 lbs. |
| Bacon | 11 lbs. | Lettuce | 12 lbs. |
| Milk | 9 lbs. | Pork & Beans | 24 lbs. |
| Tomatoes, tnd | 7 lbs. | Beef Chuck, B&R | 20 lbs. |
| Pepper, green | 1 lbs. | Onions | 4 lbs. |
| Rice | 5 lbs. | Shortening | 2 lbs. |
| Beans, string, td | 7 lbs. | Apples | 14 lbs. |
| Peas, tnd | 3 lbs. | Potatoes | 15 lbs. |
| Sausage, liver | 5 lbs. | | |

- 1 -

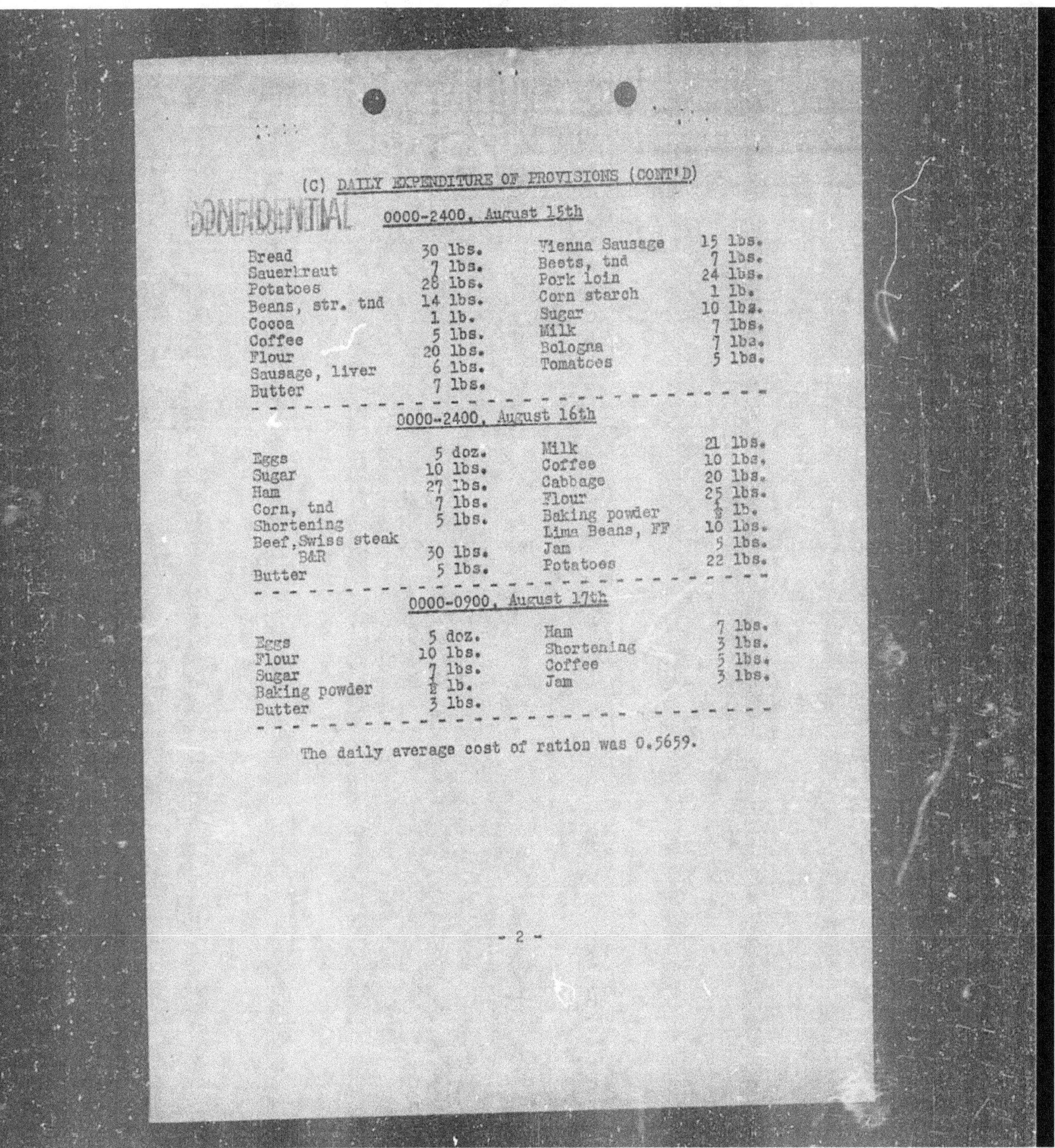

(C) DAILY EXPENDITURE OF PROVISIONS (CONT'D)



0000-2400, August 15th

| | | | |
|---|---|---|---|
| Bread | 30 lbs. | Vienna Sausage | 15 lbs. |
| Sauerkraut | 7 lbs. | Beets, tnd | 7 lbs. |
| Potatoes | 28 lbs. | Pork loin | 24 lbs. |
| Beans, str. tnd | 14 lbs. | Corn starch | 1 lb. |
| Cocoa | 1 lb. | Sugar | 10 lbs. |
| Coffee | 5 lbs. | Milk | 7 lbs. |
| Flour | 20 lbs. | Bologna | 7 lbs. |
| Sausage, liver | 6 lbs. | Tomatoes | 5 lbs. |
| Butter | 7 lbs. | | |

0000-2400, August 16th

| | | | |
|---|---|---|---|
| Eggs | 5 doz. | Milk | 21 lbs. |
| Sugar | 10 lbs. | Coffee | 10 lbs. |
| Ham | 27 lbs. | Cabbage | 20 lbs. |
| Corn, tnd | 7 lbs. | Flour | 25 lbs. |
| Shortening | 5 lbs. | Baking powder | ½ lb. |
| Beef, Swiss steak B&R | 30 lbs. | Lima Beans, FF | 10 lbs. |
| Butter | 5 lbs. | Jam | 5 lbs. |
| | | Potatoes | 22 lbs. |

0000-0900, August 17th

| | | | |
|---|---|---|---|
| Eggs | 5 doz. | Ham | 7 lbs. |
| Flour | 10 lbs. | Shortening | 3 lbs. |
| Sugar | 7 lbs. | Coffee | 5 lbs. |
| Baking powder | ½ lb. | Jam | 3 lbs. |
| Butter | 3 lbs. | | |

The daily average cost of ration was 0.5659.

- 2 -

1st copy

U.S.S. S-26



January 21, 1942.
MAR 1 1942

From: Commanding Officer.
To : Commander Submarine Division Fifty-One.

Subject: Report of War Patrol - Period 31 December 1941 to 16 January 1942.

Reference: Comsuboffshopatpac Secret Operation Order 5-41 of 27 December 1941.



1. In accordance with reference (a) this vessel proceeded on war patrol in Pacific waters off Panama on 31 December 1941. Effected transit of Panama Canal 31 December 1941, joined escort vessel, DD 247, at Balboa and proceeded to sea on course 147° in company with escort vessel, U.S.S. S-21, S-29, and S-47. At 1800 a 25 minute trim dive was made. At 1830 vessels in company set course 195° T, speed 10 knots, proceeding to a point 12 miles due west of Cape Mala.

2. Escort was released at a point about 40 miles south of Cape Mala at 0840 on January 1, 1942. U.S.S. S-21, S-26, S-29, and S-47 proceeded in company to point Cast on course 270° T. At 1800 submarines arrived at point Cast and set courses for individual patrol stations. S-26 changed course to 266° T.

3. Arrived on patrol station, latitude 6 - 30 N, Longitude 93 - 00 W at 1800 January 4, 1942, and began patrolling on courses north and south at speed 6 knots employing zigzag courses. at 0500 changed base course to 270° T. While on station patrol was conducted at 6 knots (2/3 speed on one engine), on the surface, patrolling to the west from the 93rd meridian during daylight and retiring to the east during darkness. Zigzag courses were employed both day and night. Diving was resorted to in order to avoid detection by ships. This was necessary in only one instance, on 8 January 1942, when a small merchant steamer was sighted; identity unknown. Daily section dives were conducted for training purposes and to trim the boat. Two night dives were made for training. Left patrol station at 0100, January 12, 1942, to return to base. Set course 088° T, speed 10 knots to pass through points Cast and Baker At 1315 on January 15, 1942, fell in with S-21 at point Baker. Proceeded in company on course 024° T toward rendezvous with surface escort (15 miles west of San Jose light), adjusting speed to arrive at 0700 on 16 January. At 0608 sighted escort vessel, PC 460. At 0720, S-29 joined formation. Vessels in company formed column, set course 352° T, speed 10 knots, for Balboa. 1150 escort vessel released. Transited canal on 16 January 1942. Arrived Submarine Base, Coco Solo, 2310, January 16, 1942.



-1-

CONFIDENTIAL U.S.S. S-26

Subject: Report of War Patrol - Period 31 December 1941 to 16 January 1942.

---

4. SUMMARY OF EVENTS

Wednesday, 31 Dec. 1941 -
0545 Underway from Colon Harbor to transit canal.

Thursday, 1 Jan. 1942 -
0840 Escort vessel left formation.
0955 Sighted navy patrol plane.
1028 Exchanged recognition signals with Army 4 motored bomber.

Sunday, 4 Jan -
1800 Arrived at patrol line.

Tuesday, 6 Jan -
1128 Sighted navy patrol plane 2 miles to port. Exchanged recognition signals and calls.

Wednesday, 7 Jan -
1100 Sighted navy patrol plane distance 5 miles on westerly course. No signals exchanged.

Thursday, 8 Jan -
0815 Sighted merchant ship distance 6 miles bearing 190° T on easterly course. Dove to avoid sighting. Closed track. At 0858 ship disappeared in rain squall on course 080° T, speed 8 knots, range 6000 yards, 90° port angle on bow. Ship not flying colors and not identified. About 3000 ton three island type freighter. 0947 surfaced. Sent contact report to Comsubron 3.

Friday, 9 Jan -
1048 Sighted navy patrol plane 4 miles distant. No signals exchanged.

Saturday, 10 Jan -
1015 Sighted navy patrol plane. Plane circled ship three times close aboard. Recognition signals exchanged.

Monday, 12 Jan -
0100 Left patrol line to return to Base.

Thursday, 15 Jan -
1115 Sighted navy patrol plane distant 4 miles. No signals exchanged.
1315 Fell in with S-21.

Friday, 16 Jan -
0620 Effected rendezvous with escort vessel, PC 460. Transited canal. Arrived S/M Base, Coco Solo, 2310.

-2-

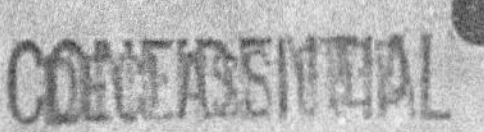

CONFIDENTIAL U.S.S. S-26

Subject: Report of War Patrol - Period 31 December 1941 to 16 January 1942.

- - - - - - - - - - - - - - - - - - - - - - - - - - - - - - - - - - - -

5. No enemy ships or planes were sighted.

6. Daily inspection of torpedoes was made. Torpedo tubes were not flooded. No defects, leaks or other material failures occured to torpedoes.

7. In general the weather was excellent. Prevailing wind was from NE accompanied by heavy ground swells.also from NE. However, most of the time there were not enough white caps to have made an undetected periscope approach possible. Current was found to be unpredictable, and changeable but a north or notheasterly set with a drift of about 1 knot was experienced most frequently. Had a full moon the entire first night on patrol (12 Jan). Thereafter the period of moonlight decreased by approximately an hour each night.

8. The habitability of the boat was very good. The air conditioning plant was in continuous operation. The temperatures of the forward battery compartment was maintained at about 70° F. With 44 men on board and only 31 bunks the "hot bunk" system was used.

9. The health and morale of the crew were excellent. No sickness or accidents occured.

10. Comments:

Radio communication 4155 kcs during the daytime was impossible but good at night. Communication on 8530 kcs was very good during the day. As no crystal was provided for 8530 kcs the "zero beat" method was used to get on frequency. No opportunity was afforded for testing sound conditions.

A dense layer of water was found to exist from a depth of 80 to 120 feet. Balancing at this depth range was found to be comparatively simple.

A considerable temperature gradient was noted as follows:

| Depth | Temperature |
|---|---|
| Surface | 84° F. |
| 43 feet | 82° |
| 80 Feet | 81° |
| 120 feet | 73 to 76° |
| 150 feet | 68° |

-3-

U.S.S. S-26

Subject: Report of War Patrol - Period 31 December 1941 to 16 January 1942.

- - - - - - - - - - - - - - - - - - - - - - - - - - - - - - - -

10. (Continued)

On five of the eight days on the patrol line, navy patrol planes were sighted. In two cases recognition signals were exchanged by flashing light. In the other three cases the planes did not approach within signalling distance.

Adequate provisions were carried for 26 days in all items except potatoes, eggs, and bread. The potatoes lasted 14 days, eggs 16 days. Bread was baked every night after the 8th day.

E. C. Hawk

E. C. HAWK.

U.S.S. S-26

| DATE | 31 Dec | 1 Jan | 2 Jan | 3 Jan | 4Jan | 5 Jan | 6 Jan | 7 Jan |
|---|---|---|---|---|---|---|---|---|
| Fuel Used | 450 | 1230 | 1200 | 1200 | 1030 | 440 | 490 | 550 |
| Fuel on hand 2400 | 27,415 | 26,185 | 24,985 | 23,785 | 22,755 | 22,315 | 21,825 | 21,275 |
| Lub. Used. | 109 | 180 | 176 | 180 | 42 | 48 | 40 | 39 |
| Lub on hand 2400 | 2586 | 2406 | 2230 | 2050 | 2018 | 1970 | 1930 | 1891 |
| Fresh Water Used | 164 | 214 | 204 | 254 | 334 | 140 | 204 | 213 |
| Water Distilled. | 70 | 196 | 154 | 194 | 154 | 210 | 224 | 353 |
| Water on hand 2400 | 895 | 910 | 860 | 800 | 620 | 690 | 710 | 850 |
| Hours C&R A.C. Run. | 9:55 | 0 | 0 | 5:36 | 0 | 8:03 | 0 | 6:15 |
| Battery Water Used | 0 | 0 | 0 | 0 | 0 | 0 | 0 | 0 |
| Battery Water on hand 2400 | 873 | 873 | 873 | 873 | 873 | 873 | 873 | 873 |
| Provisions on hand. (Fresh) | | | | | | | | |
| (Days)(Dry) | | | | | | | | |

U.S.S. S-26

| DATE | 8 Jan | 9 Jan | 10 Jan | 11 Jan | 12 Jan | 13 Jan | 14 Jan | 15 Jan |
|---|---|---|---|---|---|---|---|---|
| Fuel Used | 520 | 520 | 590 | 740 | 1160 | 1010 | 1130 | 750 |
| Fuel on hand 2400 | 20,755 | 20,235 | 19,645 | 18,905 | 17,745 | 16,735 | 15,605 | 14,855 |
| Lub. Used. | 39 | 79 | 40 | 118 | 139 | 112 | 103 | 70 |
| Lub on hand 2400 | 1852 | 1773 | 1733 | 1615 | 1476 | 1364 | 1261 | 1191 |
| Fresh Water Used | 222 | 210 | 271 | 241 | 218 | 236 | 334 | 210 |
| Water Distilled. | 322 | 190 | 196 | 336 | 238 | 136 | 434 | 0 |
| Water on hand 2400 | 950 | 930 | 855 | 950 | 970 | 870 | 970 | 760 |
| Hours C&R A.C. Run. | 0 | 2:40 | 0 | 0 | 0m | 0 | 0 | 6:22 |
| Battery Water Used | 0 | 246 | 0 | 0 | 0 | 0 | 0 | 0 |
| Battery Water on hand 2400 | 873 | 627 | 627 | 627 | 627 | 627 | 627 | 627 |
| Provisions on hand. (Fresh) | | | | | | | | |
| (Days)(Dry) | | | | | | | | |

U.S.S. S-26

| DATE | 16 Jan | | | | | | | |
|---|---|---|---|---|---|---|---|---|
| Fuel Used | 550 | | | | | | | |
| Fuel on hand 2400 | 14,305 | | | | | | | |
| Lub. Used. | 22 | | | | | | | |
| Lub on hand 2400 | 1169 | | | | | | | |
| Fresh Water Used | 260 | | | | | | | |
| Water Distilled. | 0 | | | | | | | |
| Water on hand 2400 | 500 | | | | | | | |
| Hours C&R A.C. Run. | 0 | | | | | | | |
| Battery Water Used | 0 | | | | | | | |
| Battery Water on hand 2400 | 627 | | | | | | | |
| Provisions on hand. (Fresh) | | | | | | | | |
| (Days)(Dry) | | | | | | | | |

NOTE: Plenty of provisions were carried for the trip. Upon the return at least 10 days provisions remained with the exception of having no potatoes or eggs. Bread was baked every night after the 8th day.

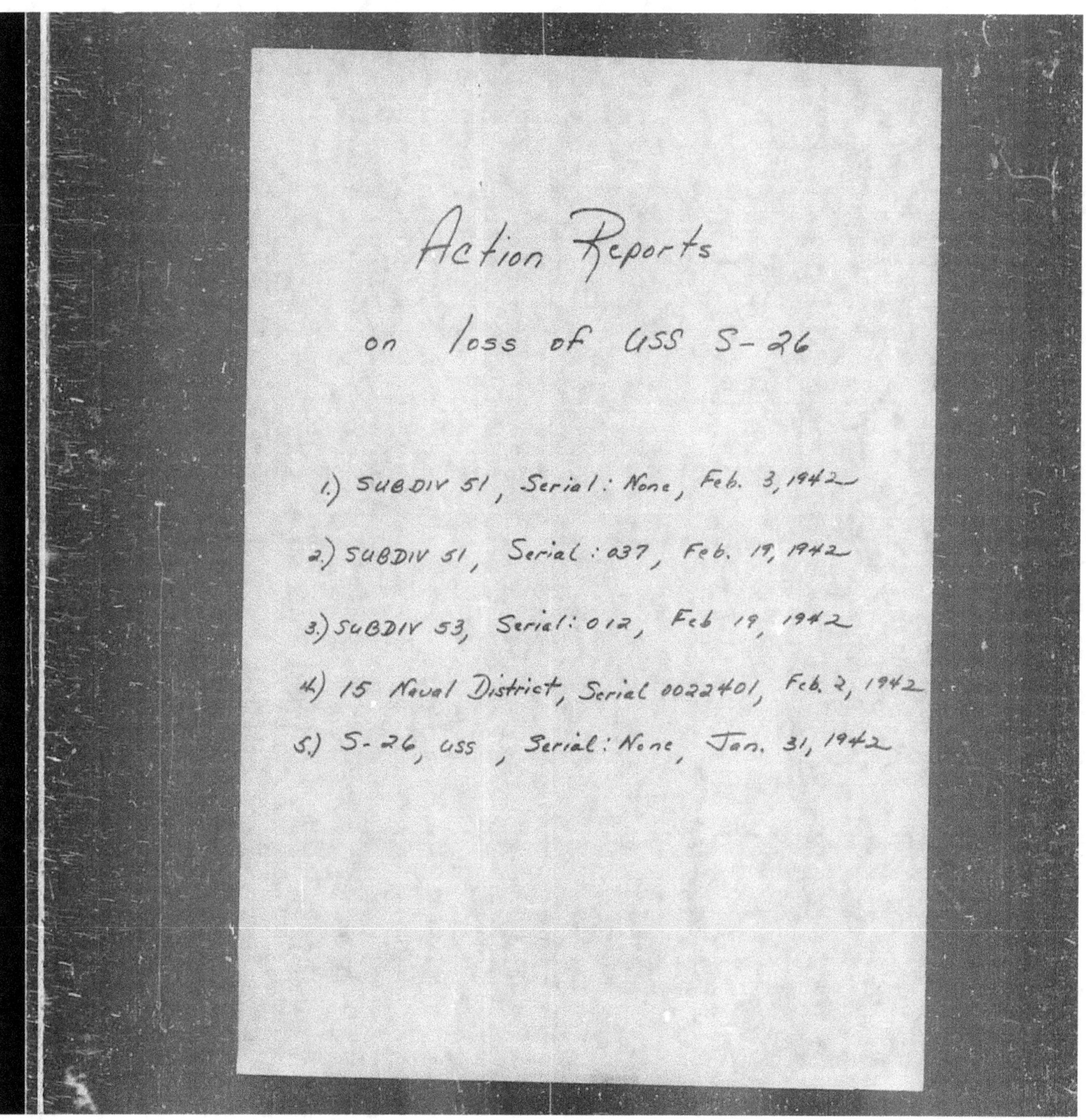

Action Reports

on loss of USS S-26

1.) SUBDIV 51, Serial: None, Feb. 3, 1942

2.) SUBDIV 51, Serial: 037, Feb. 19, 1942

3.) SUBDIV 53, Serial: 012, Feb 19, 1942

4.) 15 Naval District, Serial 0022401, Feb. 2, 1942

5.) S-26, USS, Serial: None, Jan. 31, 1942

# S-26 (SS 131)

S-26 (Lt. Cdr. E. C. Hawk) was lost at 2223 on 24 January 1942 in the Gulf of Panama about fourteen miles west of San Jose Light in three hundred feet of water. There were three survivors, two officers including the Commanding Officer, and one enlisted man—all on the bridge at the time of the collision; the fourth person on the bridge, an enlisted man, was lost.

S-26 was proceeding from Balboa, C. Z., to its patrol station in company with S-21, S-29 and S-44 and an escort vessel, PC-460, at the time of the disaster. At 2210 the escort vessel sent a visual message to the submarines that she was leaving the formation and that they could proceed on the duty assigned. S-21 was the only submarine to receive this message. Shortly thereafter PC-460 struck S-26 on the starboard side of the torpedo room and the submarine sank within a few seconds.

Salvage operations started immediately under Captain T. J. Doyle, USN, Commanding Submarine Squadron Three and Submarine Base, Coco Solo, Canal Zone; they were not successful. She had previously made one war patrol but had inflicted no damage on the enemy.



E. C. Hawk

17

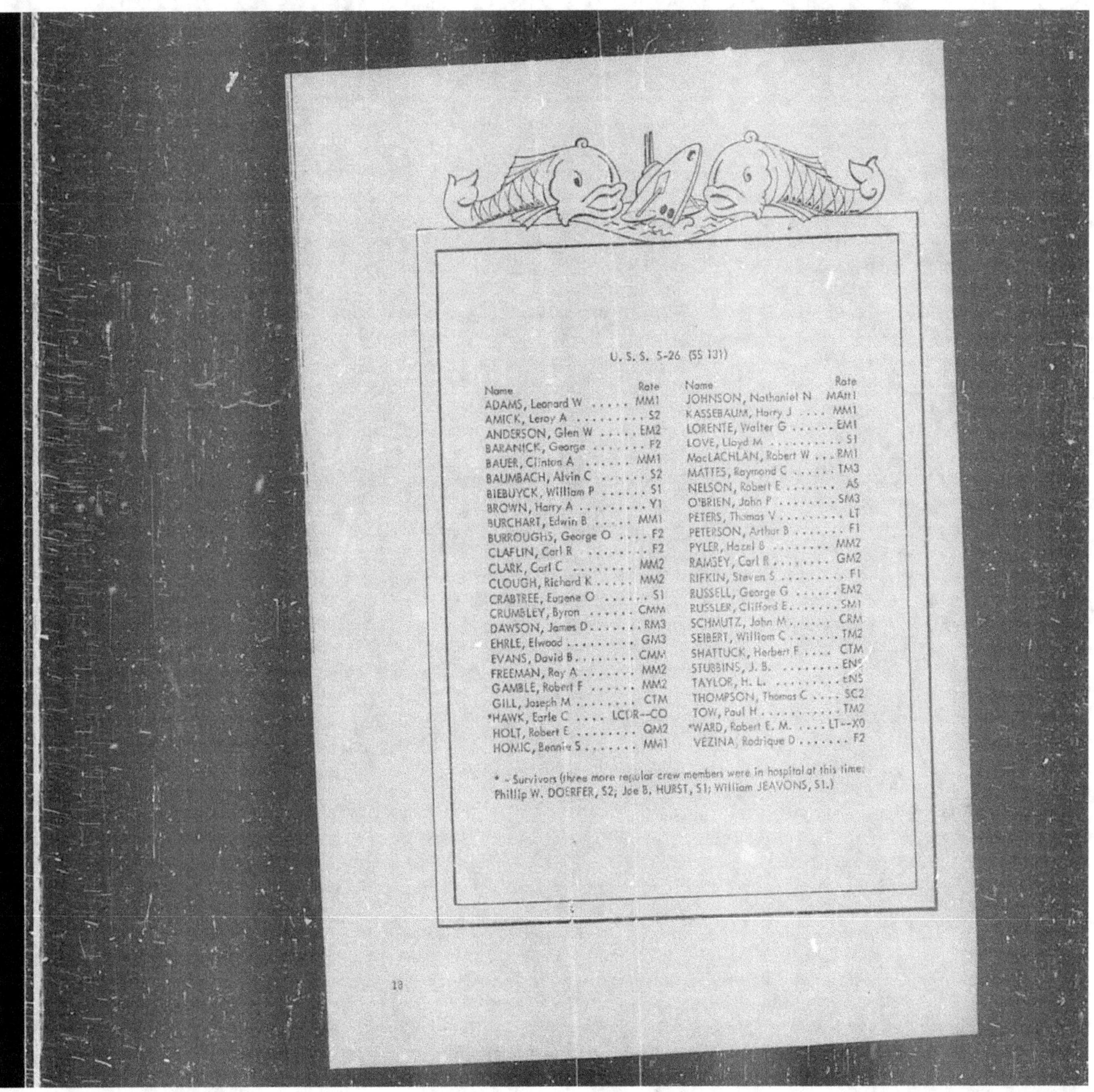

U. S. S. S-26 (SS 131)

| Name | Rate | Name | Rate |
|---|---|---|---|
| ADAMS, Leonard W ...... | MM1 | JOHNSON, Nathaniel N | MAtt1 |
| AMICK, Leroy A .......... | S2 | KASSEBAUM, Harry J .... | MM1 |
| ANDERSON, Glen W ...... | EM2 | LORENTE, Walter G ....... | EM1 |
| BARANICK, George ........ | F2 | LOVE, Lloyd M ........... | S1 |
| BAUER, Clinton A ....... | MM1 | MacLACHLAN, Robert W ... | RM1 |
| BAUMBACH, Alvin C ....... | S2 | MATTES, Raymond C ....... | TM3 |
| BIEBUYCK, William P ....... | S1 | NELSON, Robert E ........ | AS |
| BROWN, Harry A .......... | Y1 | O'BRIEN, John P ........ | SM3 |
| BURCHART, Edwin B ...... | MM1 | PETERS, Thomas V .......... | LT |
| BURROUGHS, George O ..... | F2 | PETERSON, Arthur B ....... | F1 |
| CLAFLIN, Carl R ......... | F2 | PYLER, Hazel B ......... | MM2 |
| CLARK, Carl C .......... | MM2 | RAMSEY, Carl R ......... | GM2 |
| CLOUGH, Richard K ...... | MM2 | RIFKIN, Steven S .......... | F1 |
| CRABTREE, Eugene O ....... | S1 | RUSSELL, George G ....... | EM2 |
| CRUMBLEY, Byron ....... | CMM | RUSSLER, Clifford E....... | SM1 |
| DAWSON, James D........ | RM3 | SCHMUTZ, John M ....... | CRM |
| EHRLE, Elwood .......... | GM3 | SEIBERT, William C ........ | TM2 |
| EVANS, David B......... | CMM | SHATTUCK, Herbert F .... | CTM |
| FREEMAN, Ray A ........ | MM2 | STUBBINS, J. B. ......... | ENS |
| GAMBLE, Robert F ....... | MM2 | TAYLOR, H. L. .......... | ENS |
| GILL, Joseph M ......... | CTM | THOMPSON, Thomas C .... | SC2 |
| *HAWK, Earle C .... | LCDR--CO | TOW, Paul H ............ | TM2 |
| HOLT, Robert E .......... | QM2 | *WARD, Robert E. M. .... | LT--XO |
| HOMIC, Bennie S ........ | MM1 | VEZINA, Rodrique D ........ | F2 |

* - Survivors (three more regular crew members were in hospital at this time: Phillip W. DOERFER, S2; Joe B. HURST, S1; William JEAVONS, S1.)

18

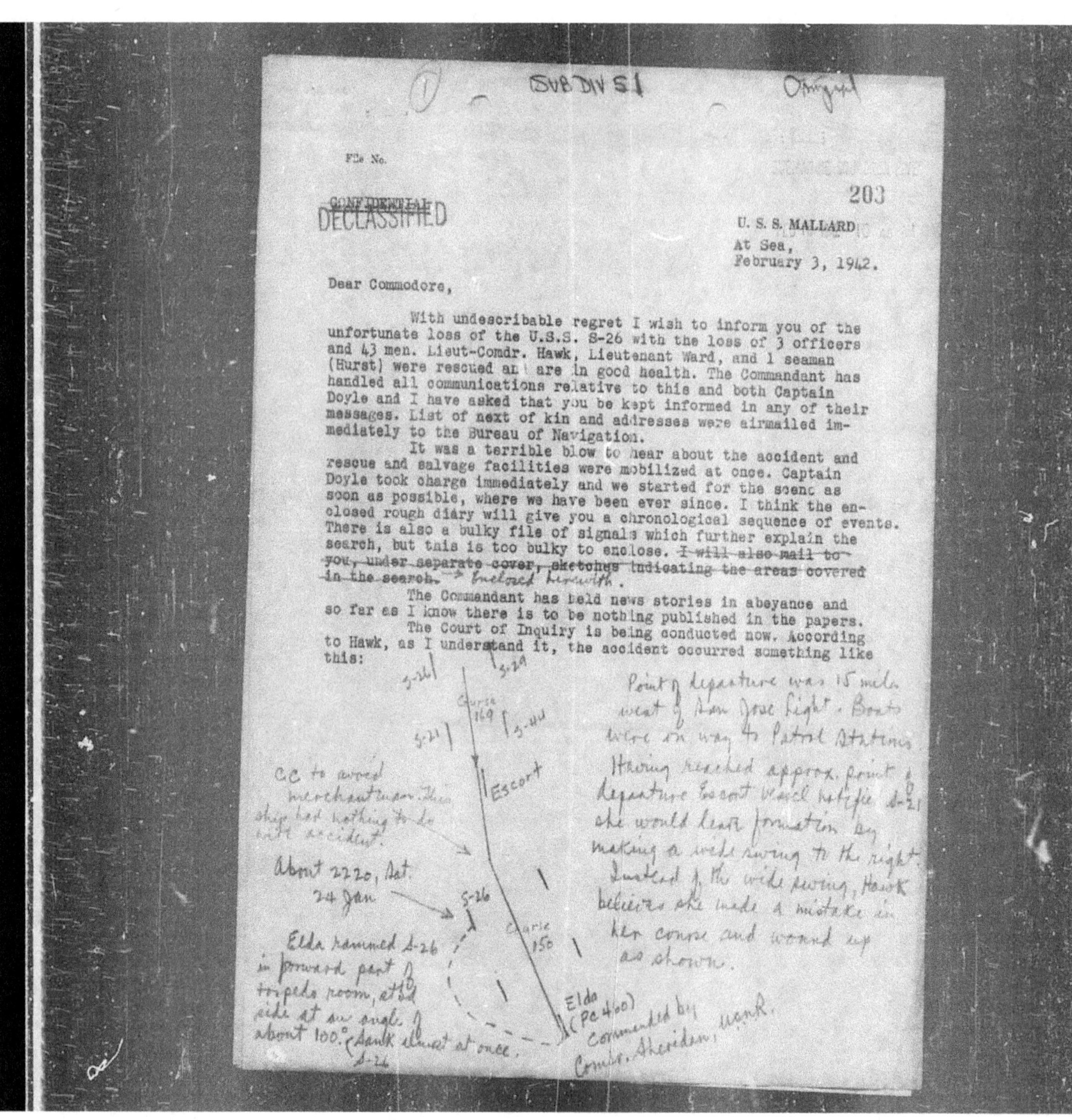

SUB DIV 51 — Original

File No.

~~CONFIDENTIAL~~ DECLASSIFIED

203

U. S. S. MALLARD
At Sea,
February 3, 1942.

Dear Commodore,

With undescribable regret I wish to inform you of the unfortunate loss of the U.S.S. S-26 with the loss of 3 officers and 43 men. Lieut-Comdr. Hawk, Lieutenant Ward, and 1 seaman (Hurst) were rescued and are in good health. The Commandant has handled all communications relative to this and both Captain Doyle and I have asked that you be kept informed in any of their messages. List of next of kin and addresses were airmailed immediately to the Bureau of Navigation.

It was a terrible blow to hear about the accident and rescue and salvage facilities were mobilized at once. Captain Doyle took charge immediately and we started for the scene as soon as possible, where we have been ever since. I think the enclosed rough diary will give you a chronological sequence of events. There is also a bulky file of signals which further explain the search, but this is too bulky to enclose. ~~I will also mail to you, under separate cover, sketches indicating the areas covered in the search.~~ Enclosed herewith.

The Commandant has held news stories in abeyance and so far as I know there is to be nothing published in the papers.

The Court of Inquiry is being conducted now. According to Hawk, as I understand it, the accident occurred something like this:

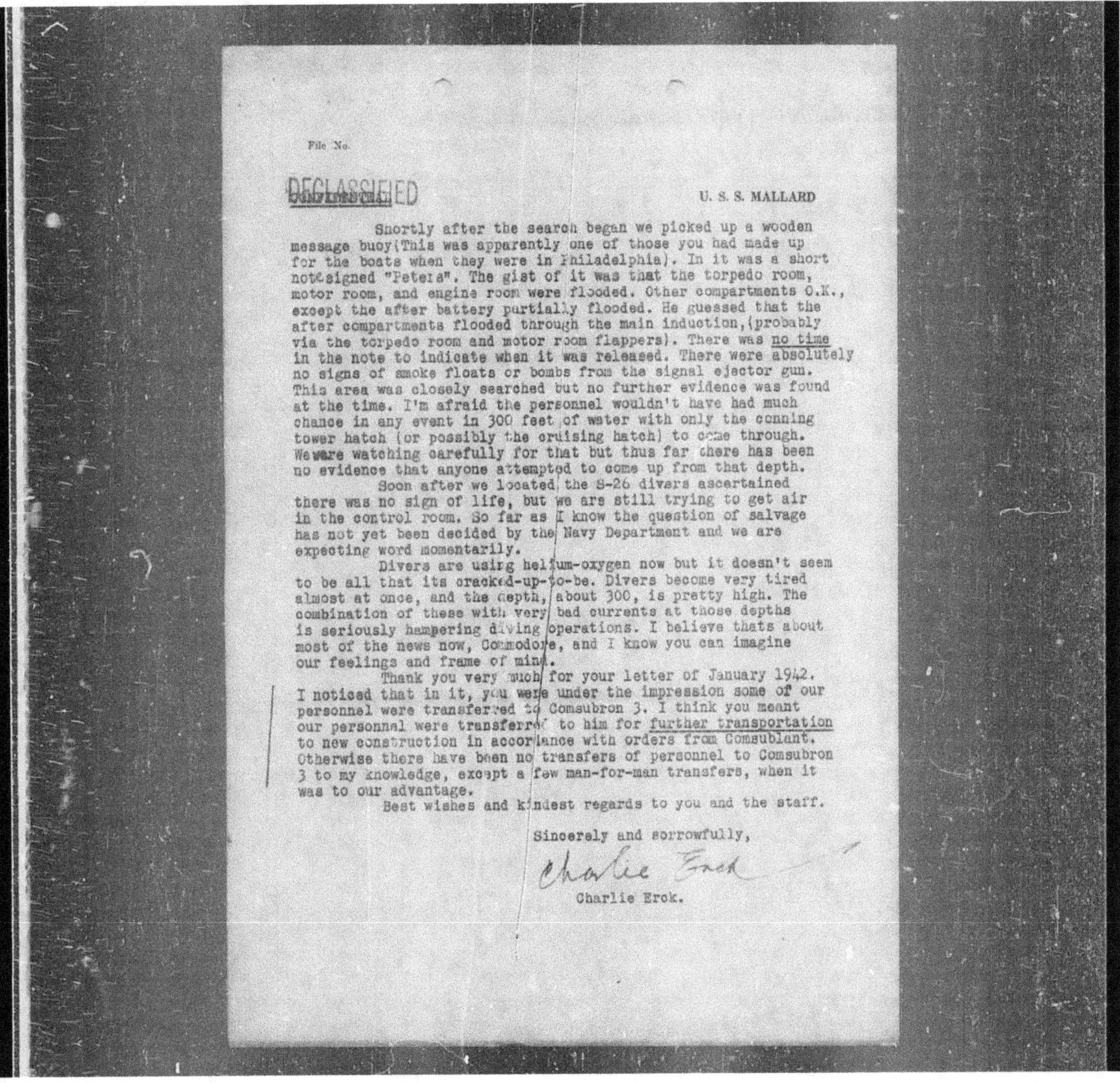

File No.

DECLASSIFIED

U. S. S. MALLARD

Shortly after the search began we picked up a wooden message buoy (This was apparently one of those you had made up for the boats when they were in Philadelphia). In it was a short note signed "Peters". The gist of it was that the torpedo room, motor room, and engine room were flooded. Other compartments O.K., except the after battery partially flooded. He guessed that the after compartments flooded through the main induction, (probably via the torpedo room and motor room flappers). There was no time in the note to indicate when it was released. There were absolutely no signs of smoke floats or bombs from the signal ejector gun. This area was closely searched but no further evidence was found at the time. I'm afraid the personnel wouldn't have had much chance in any event in 300 feet of water with only the conning tower hatch (or possibly the cruising hatch) to come through. We were watching carefully for that but thus far there has been no evidence that anyone attempted to come up from that depth.

Soon after we located the S-26 divers ascertained there was no sign of life, but we are still trying to get air in the control room. So far as I know the question of salvage has not yet been decided by the Navy Department and we are expecting word momentarily.

Divers are using helium-oxygen now but it doesn't seem to be all that its cracked-up-to-be. Divers become very tired almost at once, and the depth, about 300, is pretty high. The combination of these with very bad currents at those depths is seriously hampering diving operations. I believe thats about most of the news now, Commodore, and I know you can imagine our feelings and frame of mind.

Thank you very much for your letter of January 1942. I noticed that in it, you were under the impression some of our personnel were transferred to Comsubron 3. I think you meant our personnel were transferred to him for further transportation to new construction in accordance with orders from Comsublant. Otherwise there have been no transfers of personnel to Comsubron 3 to my knowledge, except a few man-for-man transfers, when it was to our advantage.

Best wishes and kindest regards to you and the staff.

Sincerely and sorrowfully,

Charlie Erck

Charlie Erck.

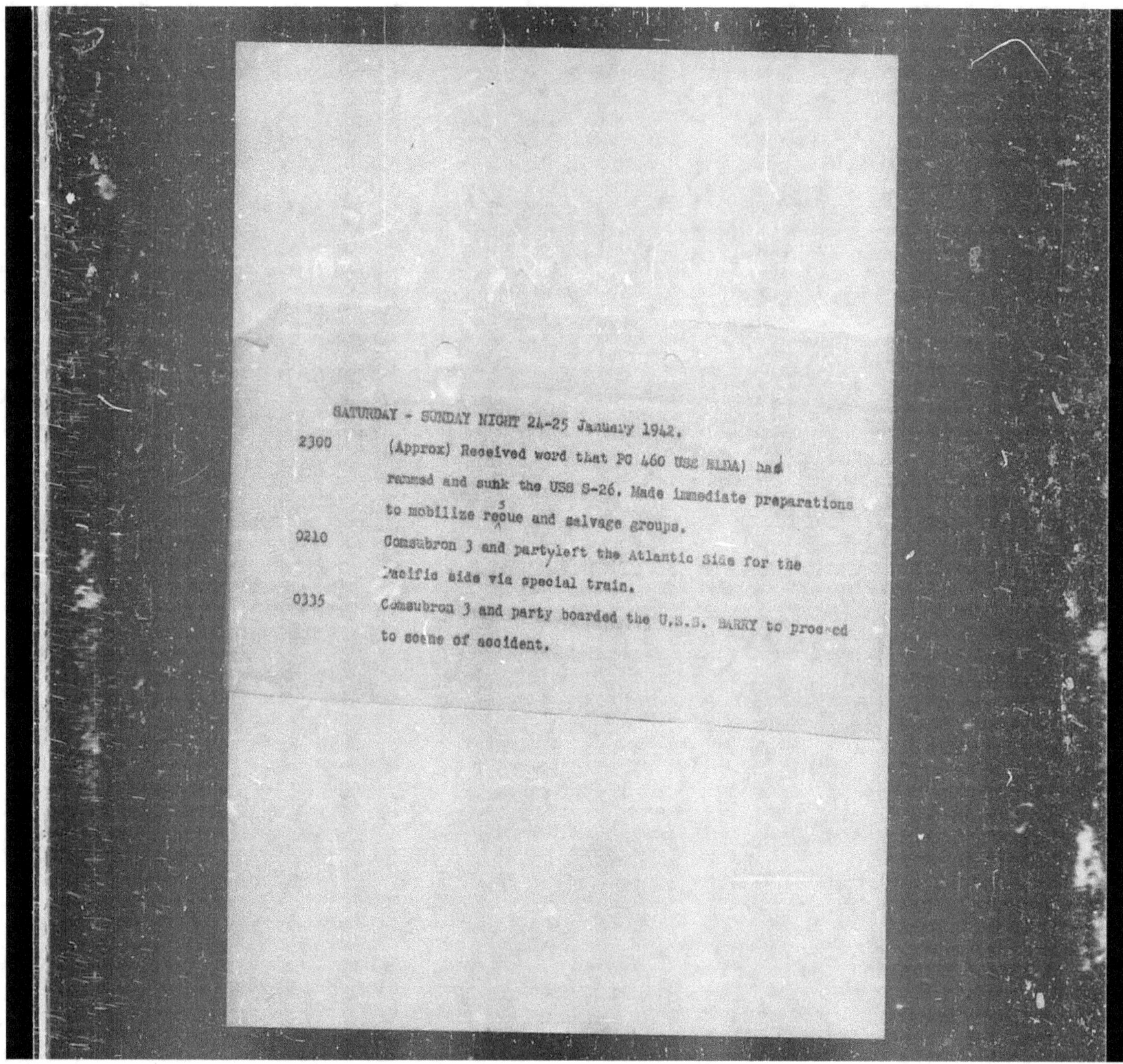

SATURDAY - SUNDAY NIGHT 24-25 January 1942.

2300 (Approx) Received word that PC 460 USS ELDA) has rammed and sunk the USS S-26. Made immediate preparations to mobilize rescue and salvage groups.

0210 Comsubron 3 and party left the Atlantic Side for the Pacific side via special train.

0335 Comsubron 3 and party boarded the U.S.S. BARRY to proceed to scene of accident.

U.S.S. S-26 - Submarine Search and Salvage Operations.
U.S.S. BARRY - Sunday, 25 January, 1942

0025 Made preparations for getting underway.

0300 Stationed special sea detail.

0335 Comsubron 3 and party came aboard.

0350 Underway. Steering various courses and making various speeds.

0400 Underway as before. Speed 15 knots.

0446 Changed speed to 25. Changed course to 150 T.

0458 Changed course to 171 T.

0535 Exchanged calls with PC 450.

0600 Exchanged calls with Elda (PC 460)

0610 Changed speed to 15.

0618 Changed speed to 20.

0630 Changed speed to 15.

0631 Exchanged calls with S-21.

0635 Changed speed to 10.

0641 Exchanged calls with S-29.

0645 Stopped. Laying to in company with Elda, S-21, S-29, S-44 and Tuna Clipper Monte Bianco.

0650 Motor whale boat left the ship for Elda.

0700 Motor whale boat returned to ship with Commanding Officer Elda and 3 survivors of the S-26. Comsubron 3 conducted conference with these personnel and determined approximate location of accident. This was difficult because of unpredictable strong currents in this area and a blackout of navigational aids.

0745 Commanding Officer, Elda left the ship.

0801 Motor whale boat returned to the ship.

0830 Motor whale boat left the ship for the Elda.

-1-

U.S.S. S-26 - Submarine Search and Salvage Operations.
U.S.S. BARRY - Sunday, 25 January, 1942 (Contd).

0837 Motor whale boat alongside with Commanding Officer of the Elda, (PC 460).

0842 Motor whale boat returned to the Elda(PC 460).

0845 The U.S.S. S-21, S-29, and S-44 taking position for search.

0853 Vessel sighted bearing 349 T. Identified as USS WOODCOCK.

0858 USS WOODCOCK reported for duty with Comsubron 3.

0900 Went ahead at 6 knots to ass me guide for searching line.

0904 Getting in position on search line. Changed course to 359 T.

0907 Changed course to 349 T.

0908 Changed course to 359 T.

0910 Changed course to 019 T.

0912 Stopped all engines.

0914 Changed speed to 6. Changed course to 359 T. Line formed just ahead of Tuna Clipper and continued search.

0920 Army plane approaching close from south. Flying due north. U.S.S. WOODCOCK maneuvering into search line.

0930 Sighted yellow object 100 yards broad on beam.

0930 Both engines stopped.

0931 Both engines backing 1/3 - 5 knots.

0935 Both engines stopped.

0939 Starboard engine ahead 2/3 - 10 knots.

0939 Port engine backing 1/3 - 5 knots.

0941 Both engines stopped.

0950 Gig left the ship to inspect yellow object. Lt[illegible]
([illegible]

-2-

U.S.S. S-26 - Submarine Search and Salvage Operations.
U.S.S. BARRY - Sunday, 25 January, 1942 (Con't).

| | |
|---|---|
| 0955 | Lieut. Ward in gig / Picked up yellow buoy and returned to ship. This buoy contained a message from the sunken submarine. |
| 0955 | Recalled motor whale boat / continued search. |
| 1007 | Exchanged calls with USS SAMPSON. |
| 1010 | Changed speed to 5. Changed course to 359 T. |
| 1013 | Changed course to 314 T. Sighted what appeared to be a slick to the northward. |
| 1020 | USS SAMPSON reporting for duty ready to assist in search with supersonic fathometer and started sound search in the immediate area. |
| 1021 | Changed course to 349 T. and ran along slick. |
| 1027 | Changed course to 350 T. |
| 1037 | Sighted what appeared to be another yellow buoy bearing 262 T. |
| 1038 | Two objects now visible on same bearing. |
| 1040 | Stopped all engines. Speed zero. Lowered boats, / Planted marker buoy. and searched area. Buoy planted at northern limit of slick |
| 1045 | S-21 investigating objects sighted. |
| 1047 | Objects identified as three empty boxes. Negative evidence. |
| 1049 | Motor whale boat returned to the ship. All ships maneuvering on various courses and at varying speeds while searching. |
| 1055 | Motor Whale boat left the ship with crew and grapnel handling party. Mr. Gibbs in charge. Dragged in this area. |
| 1057 | Navy patrol plane flying low, passing from south to north. |
| 1100 | Patrol plane circling area. |
| 1115 | Maneuvering into position to resume search. |
| 1119 | ~~Lieutenant, Bell~~ Commanding Officer SAMPSON reported aboard. Gig lying off. |

-3-

U.S.S. S-26 - Submarine Search and Salvage Operations.
U.S.S. BARRY - Sunday, 25 January 1942(Contd)

1212 USS SAMPSON gig tied up alongside BARRY.

1218 USS SAMPSON gig shoved off to lie off with other boats.

1219 Changed course to 25. Investigating oil slick reported by SAMPSON. Other ships various courses and speeds.

NOTE: SAMPSON has reported oil slicks which she is investigating to the southwestward. We later joined her to take a sample of the oil and we believe it to be diesel.

1223 Changed course to 199 T.

1229 Freighter sighted bearing 224 T.

1235 Changed speed to 20.

1243 Changed speed to 10.

1245 Stopped all engines.

1304 Sighted can in water bearing 315 T., distance approximately 300 yards.

1306 USS SAMPSON boat approaching ship for ~~Captain Bell~~ (CO SAMPSON).

1307 BARRY's gig left ship with party in charge of Ens. Coolidge to investigate can sighted.

1314 Gig returned to ship with can - cigarette can containing no identification data. Gig shoved off to pick up line floating astern. Negative evidence.

1316 USS SAMPSON boat alongside bringing sample of oil slicked water. Sample contains definite signs of oil - probably diesel.

1320 USS SAMPSON's boat shoved off with CO SAMPSON.

1321 Gig alongside ready for hoisting.

-4-

U.S.S. S-26 - Submarine Search and Salvage Operations.
U.S.S. BARRY - Sunday, January 25, 1942 (Contd).

1323 Gig hoisted to high rail.

1324 Changed speed to 5. Maneuvering into position astern of SAMPSON. So Sampson could continue sound search.

1337 Stopped all engines.

1342 Changed speed to 5. Maneuvering to investigate life ring and object bearing 059 T., astern of SAMPSON.

1343 Stopped all engines.

1344 Changed speed to 5.

1348 Stopped all engines.

1356 Picked up life ring. Believe it belongs to ELDA.

NOTE: (1400) Picking up life buoy apparently belonging to ELDA (PC460). This was discovered after oil slick had been sighted. Believe indicates leakage of oil immediately after last evenings collision and the ELDA's life rings which she threw overboard after the collision. Believe this shows a drift of about 1 knot per hour on about 200°

1430 USS MALLARD sighted.

1444 Changed spedd to 15.

1448 Steady on course 024 T.

1453 USS MALLARD ordered by Comsubron 3 to report to SAMPSON for orders on sound search.

1457 Changed speed to 20.

1512 Stopped all engines.

1519 Changed speed to 15.

-5-

U.S.S. S-26 - Submarine Search and Salvage Operations.
U.S.S. BARRY - Sunday, January 25, 1942 (Contd).

1531 Changed speed to 10.

1534 Changed speed to 5.

1536 All engines stopped.

1550 Changed speed to 10.

1555 All engines stopped.

1555 Comsubron 3 and party left ship for USS MALLARD.

U.S.S. MALLARD - Sunday January 25, 1942.

1600 Comsubron 3 and party reported on board. Ships maneuvering at various courses and speeds continuing search.

1720 Mallard commenced sweeping with magnetic sweep using two motor surf boats.

Note: During early evening SAMPSON reported sound contacts and buoyed spot.

2105 Ceased magnetic sweeping. Sent boats to drag instead for objects, by grapnel so that sensitive mike might be used.

2115 USS SAMPSON buoy apparently stopped watching. Whaleboats and USS SAMPSON boats working together to develope contacts.

2230 MALLARD small boat drag hooked heavy strain.

2235 USS SAMPSON pinging and sensitive mike working - No results.

2256 Ahead std speed, course 045 mag.

2302 Stopped. Lying to - Ships heading 85 mag.

2340 Ahead 1/3.

MONDAY, January 26, 1942.

0025 Ahead 1/3. Various courses and speeds maintaining search.

0030 Engine stopped.

0105 Ahead 1/3 - course 210 mag.

-6-

U.S.S. S-26 - Submarine Search and Salvage Operations.
U.S.S. MALLARD, Monday, January 26, 1942.

0130 Compass reading 272 mag.

0153 Changed course to 320 mag.

0230 Hoisted in motor whale boat.

0255 Hoisted in 2nd motor whale boat.

0531 Changed course to 180 mag.

0607 Changed course to 270 mag.

0625 Changed course to 000 mag.

0715 Changed course to 220 mag.

0745 Stopped.

0740 Canal ship Favorite arrived.

0740 USS MALLARD received stores from FAVORITE.

0750 Motor whale boat in water.

0815 2nd motor whale boat in water.

NOTE: USS WOODCOCK dragging by grapnel.

0840 Ahead 1/3 - various courses and various speeds for all ships maintaining search.

0844 Stopped. Ships heading 155.

0850 Ahead 1/3. Changed course to 225 mag. MALLARD continued sweeping operations with magnetic drag streamed between two motor surf boats.

0955 The following men reported aboard from the Experimental Diving Unit, Washington Navy Yard, Wash. D.C. SQUIRE, W.H. CTM. SMITH, F.E. CEM. CROCKER, G. EMlc., SHAHAN, N.C. EMlc., GRIFFIN, J.E. CMlc., MASON, G.E. GMlc.
Also Press representatives came aboard.

1025 Changed course to 120 mag. Various courses and speeds for searching groups.

-7-

U.S.S.S-26 - Submarine Search and Salvage Operations.
U.S.S. MALLARD, Monday, January 26, 1942.

1030 Changed course to 060 mag.

SHIPS PRESENT

MALLARD - CSS 3.

USS WOODCOCK

US FAVORITE

SAMPSON

BARRY

S-21

S-29

S-44

TUNA CLIPPER CONTE BIANCO.

1138 Standard speed. Course 130 mag.

1145 Stopped.

1150 Changed speed to 1/3.

1151 Stopped. During searching operations it was frequently necessary for all vessels to maneuver on various courses and at various speeds while trying to develope possible contacts. Ships buoyed most likely locations or contacts. This not is applicable throughout this diary.

1200 USS SAMPSON reports possible contact - No results.

1225 Changed speed to 2/3. Right to 270 Mag.

1258 Ahead 1/3.

1305 Stopped. Heading 235 mag.

1325 Stopped. Heading 280 mag.

1331 Ahead 2/3. Dragging with WOODCOCK and FAVORITE. Formed normal line of bearing. MALLARD's small boats sweeping with magnetic sweep.

-8-

U.S.S. S-26 - Submarine Search and Salvage Operations.
U.S.S. MALLARD, Monday, January 26, 1942.

1345 Changed course to 045 mag.

1355 Changed course to 130 mag.

1405 Changed course to 225 mag.

1428 Changed course to 230 mag. Speed 1/3

1429 Speed 2/3. Course 030 mag.

1431 Standard speed.

1434 Speed 2/3

1438 Speed 1/3. Course 035.

1530 Changed course to 225 mag. Continuing dragging in company with WOODCOCK and FAVORITE.

1600 Sampson had negative contact

1650 Changed course to 150 mag.

1700 Changed course to 045 mag.

1710 Obtained book from plane. Plane had retrieved book from water. Book appeared to be a ship's service cash book. Negative evidence.

1750 Motor Torpedo Boat alongside with special magnetic gear.

1800 MALLARD took in drag. Small boats continuing to sweep with magnetic sweeps. USS SAMPSON's motor whale boat returned to SAMPSON after disembarking listening crew on MALLARD.

1800 SAMPSON and BARRY ordered to rendezvous with MALLARD.

1820 Taking in magnetic drag from MALLARD's small boats.

NOTE: Preparing special gear for dragging. Mr J.H. Glass., from 15th Naval District in charge. REED, J.L. MM2c, USN., assisting.

1905 USS SAMPSON motor whale boat came alongside to puck up Press Representatives who came aboard MALLARD this morning about 0955.

-9-

U.S.S. S-26 - Submarine Search and Salvage Operations.
U.S.S. MALLARD, Monday, January 26, 1942.

2027 Ahead 1/3. Continuing to search on various courses and at varying speeds. New type drag rigged.

2032 Ahead 2/3.

2115 Ahead 1/3

U.S.S. MALLARD, Tuesday, January 27, 1942.

0000-0400

Continuing search on various courses and at varying speeds with S-21, S-29, S-44, WOODCOCK, BARRY, SAMPSON, PC 460, FAVORITE, Comsubron 3 in MALLARD.

0415 Changed course to 270 mag.

0426 Steady course 270.

0446 Changed course to 090 mag.

0515 Changed course to 270 mag.

0545 Changed course to 090 mag.

0600 Changed course to 270 mag.

0640 Motor torpedo boat No. 6 came alongside.

0645 Sighted merchantman bearing 347.

NOTE: USS BARRACUDA, BONITA, and BOWDITCH arrived and reported for duty.

0715 Commanding Officer, U.S.S. BOWDITCH came aboard.

0730 Commanding Officer, U.S.S. BOWDITCH left the ship.

0805 Motor Whale boats put in water for magnetic drag.

US FAVORITE directed to drag in vicinity of Tuna Clipper.

MALLARD laying to. Ships heading ~~222~~.250.

0855 Press representatives came aboard from USS SAMPSON.

0900 Motor torpedo boat sighted bearing 310.

-10-

U.S.S. S-26 - Submarine Search and Salvage Operations.
U.S.S. MALLARD, Tuesday, January 27, 1942.

| | |
|---|---|
| 0910 | Motor torpedo boat came alongside with helium manifold. |
| 0959 | Motor torpedo boat shoved off. |
| 1000 | Ships heading 260 |
| 1113 | Ships heading 220, Preparing to take one end of sweep wire from WOODCOCK for sweep operations of WOODCOCK and MALLARD. |
| 1136 | Streamed sweep with USS WOODCOCK, using 1800 feet of 5/8" plow steel wire out to 350 feet of towing cable (2½ inch steel wire) on WOODCOCK and 80 fathoms of 8 inch line carrying 300 pounds weight on MALLARD. Commenced sweep operations oncourse 220 T, making 20 RPM, distance 400 yards on port beam of WOODCOCK. |
| 1200 | Continuing sweep operations with WOODCOCK. |
| 1248 | Heavy strain on sweep. Stopped engine. |
| 1249 | Ahead 1/3. |
| 1250 | Stopped. Buoy bearing 290, distance ~~xxxxx~~ 1500 yards, estimate 700 yards from Comsubron 3 plot of first day. |
| 1254 | Ahead 1/3/ |
| 1255 | Stopped. |
| 1305 | Taking in on sweep wire. |
| 1305 | Navy plane on water circling MALLARD. |
| 1307 | Navy plane took off. |
| 1310 | Ships heading 193 T. |
| 1315 | Transferred MALLARD end of sweep to WOODCOCK. |
| 1329 | USS S-21 diving. |

-11-

U.S.S. S-26 - Submarine Search and Salvage Operations.
U.S.S. MALLARD, Tuesday, January 27, 1942.

1332 Sounding alongside. 46 fathoms. Sounding discloses 285' 2" of water.

1425 Sighted smoke bomb from U.S.S. S-21, bearing 161, distance 2 miles.

1429 U.S.S. S-21 surfaced. Distance 2 miles. Negative results.

1435 Sweep wire let go from WOODCOCK. Examination for paint is negative. Buoy in position of sweep contact.

1555 USS ELDA, USS BARRY, and Tuna Clipper Conte Bianco released and directed to report to Cominshopatpac.

NOTE: USS S-29 and S-44 released and directed to report to Comsubdiv 31 for instructions.

1645 Received one end of sweep wire from WOODCOCK. Resumed sweep operations as before - course 020 - 25 turns.

NOTE: USS MALLARD's Motor whale boats hoisted in.

All vessels reported negative results thus far. Same for small boats

1825 US FAVORITE's boat came alongside - reports drag hooked on heavy object. PC 456 sent to develope contact. Later determinedthat object was probably telegraphic cable.

1841 WOODCOCK placed light on ~~their~~ her red buoy.

1900 Barracuda obtained negative results.

2000 USS WARRINGTON motor whale boat adrift. Picked up by WARRINGTON 2nd motor whale boat.

2020 Changed course to 200 T. Continuing sweep operations with WOODCOCK.

NOTE: Weather clear. Wind: force 3 from north.

2103 Passed buoy on beam to stbd of WOODCOCK.

2112 Changed course right to 250 T.

2121 Changed course to 270 T.

-12-

U.S.S. S-26 - Submarine Search and Salvage Operations.
U.S.S. MALLARD, Tuesday, January 27, 1942.

2150 (About) Distance began to close between the two ships.

2152 Sweep took heavy strain.

2153 Stopped - WOODCOCK stopped.

2200 (About) WOODCOCK commenced heaving in on sweep. Both ships commenced swinging to port.

2206 WOODCOCK reported heavy strain on sweep and commenced easing out wire to sweep.

2215 (about) Veered to 10 fathoms on sweep. WOODCOCK bow swung past stern.

2220 Ship heading 178 T.

2300 Passed sweep to WOODCOCK.

2334 Ahead 1/3.

/7/ U.S.S. MALLARD, Wednesday, January 28, 1942.

0112 Ahead on 025 T.

0130 Stopped.

0150 Ahead on various courses and varying speeds.

0620 Ahead 1/3.

0637 Stopped.

0715 British merchantman stood in and stopped. Directed to proceed.

0725 Developed object in sweep by magnetometer + sensitive mike

0735 USS WARRINGTON motor whale boat came alongside with Press Representatives.

0757 PC 456 developing same object by magnetic detector

0807 Ship heading 018 T.

NOTE: WOODCOCK is ~~anchored~~ held fast on spot where drag is caught. MALLARD motor whale boats in water dragging with magnetic drag.

0811 Ahead 1/3.

-13-

U.S.S. S-26 - Submarine Search and Salvage Operations.

U.S.S. MALLARD, Wednesday, January 28, 1942.

0814 Stopped.

0818 Ahead 2/3.

0819 Ahead 1/3.

0820 Sighted plane bearing 220.

0820 Stopped. Ship's heading north.

0840 Ship heading 260 T.

0920 USS BARRACUA and WARRINGTON making sound search to develope object held in WOODCOCK sweep.

0926 Ahead standard speed.

0940 Stopped.

0944 Motor torpedo boat came alongside with Comdt. 15th ND.

NOTE: Results of USS BARRACUA fathometer -
Following soundings obtained as bow swings X 47 & 42 X 47 & 44 X 47 & 45 X 47 X.

1048 Motor ~~[illegible]~~ torpedo boat #0 shoved off with Comdt. 15th ND.

1048 Motor torpedo boat #2 came alongside.with stores.

1054 Motor torpedo boat #2 shoved off.

1100 Continuing to develope contact made by WOODCOCK sweep.

1205 WOODCOCK buoying position of sweep contact. MALLARD motor whale boats dragging with magnetic drag. WARRINGTON and BARRACUBA continuing to develope Woodcock sweep contact.

1205 WOODCOCK commenced heaving in sweep.

1230 (about) WOODCOCK wire came in heavily coated with brass or bronze, indicating contact with S-26. Sent weighted and buoyed divers descending line to WOODCOCK.

-14-

U.S.S. S-26 - Submarine Search and Salvage Operations.
U.S.S. MALLARD, Wednesday, January 28, 1942.

1300 WOODCOCK sweep wire tending up and down. Sent divers descending line weight down sweep wire on a shackle. Sweep wire cut, because it was jammed and could not be freed. Woodcock then got clear of area

1415 In position to commence 1st run for moor.

1420 Ahead 1/3. Course 000 T.

1422 Ahead 2/3.

1425 Preparing to make two point moor in preparation for sending down diver to investigate WOODCOCK sweep contact.

1431 Stopped.

1432 Dropped one anchor and buoy. Buoy failed to watch. Preparing 2nd anchor and buoy to go over.

1455 Back 2/3.

1456 Stopped.

1527 Continuing preparations for letting go 2nd anchor and 2 buoys.

1535 Ahead standard speed.

1536 Stopped. Maneuvering for position to drop 2nd anchor and buoy.

1553 Ahead 2/3.

1600 Stopped.

1604 Ahead 2/3. Making the approach to moor. Various courses and varying speeds.

1644 Dropped anchor and buoy. Descending line buoy bearing 215.

1645 Ahead 2/3.

1659 Ahead standard speed. Maneuvering to moor.

-15-

U.S.S. S-26 - Submarine Search and Salvage Operations.
U.S.S. MALLARD, Wednesday, January 28, 1942.

1701 Ahead 1/3.

1745 Dropped stern anchor as 2nd part of two point moor.

Maneuvering at various speeds to complete moor.

1800 Moor completed. The ship then went successively into a 3-point, 4-point + finally a 5-point moor, because of strong currents + sudden gusty winds.

DIVING OPERATIONS - Wednesday, Jan 28, 1942.

1st Diver - DENISON, H.D. CMlc.,

1820 Diver dressed - phones OK.

1823 Diver going down.

1825 At 100 feet. Diver OK.

1826 At 200 feet. Diver OK.

1827 At 250 feet, ~~XXXXXXX~~. From diver: Something fouled on my hose.

1827-30 From diver: Take me up.

1829 Taking diver up to 100 feet.

1830-30 From diver: OK - hold that - slack off - hold that - slack off, I have turn under stage.

1831-30 From diver: take me up a little.

1832 From the diver: On the stage.

1832-30 To diver: What are you doing? A. I feel OK - my arms are tired. To diver: We a re going to lower stage 10 ft.

1833-45 From diver: hold stage.

1834-30 Started time.

1836 To diver: Was wire fouled around descending line? A. Yes on descending line.

-16-

U.S.S. S-26 - Submarine Search and Salvage Operations.
U.S.S. MALLARD, Wednesday, January 28, 1942.

| | |
|---|---|
| 1840 | Shifting phones. |
| 1841-30 | Up stage. |
| 1844 | New phone in commission - From diver: OK. |
| 1844-30 | Up stage. |
| 1845 | Ventilate. |
| 1846-30 | To diver: Circulate - How do you feel? |
| 1852 | From diver: OK. |
| 1854-30 | Up stage to 50 ft. |
| 1856 | From diver: I feel OK. To diver: Unshackle. |
| 1900 | Diver on deck. |
| 1902 | Diver to recompression chamber. |
| 2005 | Changing position of mooring to ~~verticalize~~ place descending line in a vertical position. |
| 2024 | 2nd diver started dressing. |
| 2145 | Diving conditions unfavorable due to wind, tide and position of ship. Shifting mooring position for more favorable diving conditions. Diving to be resumed tomorrow morning, January 29, 1942. |
| 2150 | Slipped mooring - underway. |
| 2205 | Hoisted in motor whale boat. Maneuvering at varying speeds on various courses. |
| | U.S.S. MALLARD, Thursday, January 29, 1942. |
| 0815 | Ahead at various speeds, coming to course 310, maneuvering for position to commence laying moor. |
| 0836-30 | Dropped second(single) spud, ahead standard, full left rudder, steady on 180. |

-17-

U.S.S. S-26 - Submarine Search and Salvage Operations.
U.S.S. MALLARD, Thursday, January 29, 1942.

0841 Ahead 1/3, course 160.

0833 Full left, various courses and speeds.

0849 Commenced run to drop stern anchor.

0850-30 Dropped stern anchor. for 3 point moor.

0859 Line out to single spud.

0904 Line secured to single spud.

0903-30 Line out to double spud.

0906-30 Line secured to double spud.

0912 Centered in three-point moor. Later went into 4 point, then 5 point moor.

0940 Diver dressed - phone not working - commenced working on phone.

1100 Phone in commission.

1103 Diver on stage(AGNESS, R.J. GM1c.).

1104 Diver on descending line - going down.

1106 100 ft over the side - diver OK.

1106-30 150 ft over the side - diver OK.

1107 200 ft over the side - diver OK.

1108 250 ft over the side - diver OK.

1109 300 ft over the side - diver OK.

1110 To diver: You are getting close - A. OK.

1110-30 350 ft over - diver OK.

1111 From diver: Give me slack.

1112 400 ft over the side - diver OK.

1112-15 From diver: I hit something.

1113 From diver: I am kicking on hull - am OK - Give me some slack on descending line.

-18-

U.S.S. S-26 - Submarine Search and Salvage Operations.
U.S.S. MALLARD, Thursday, January 29, 1942.

1114-30 From Diver - I am going clear to bottom.

1115 From diver: Take me up about 5 ft.

1115-15 From diver: take me up some more.

1115-30 From diver: Let descending line down - A. No.

1116-30 From diver: Are you sending light - A. No.

1118-45 To diver: Stand by to come up.

1121-30 250 ft on deck.

1122-30 200 ft on deck.

1123 On stage.

1131 Diver coming up to 90.

1135 Diver coming up to 80

1142 Diver coming up to 70.

1150 Diver coming up to 60.

1151 Ventilated.

1152 Circulated.

1207 Reached 50 ft.

U.S.S. MALLARD, Friday, January 30, 1942.

NOTE: USS MALLARD moored over position of submarine. Ship heading 357 T. Five point moor. Three points forward two points aft.

1400 Making preparations to send diver down.

DIVER - SMITH, F.E. CBM

1514 Commenced dressing diver.

1528 Phones OK.

1530 On stage - over the side.

1532 On stage - back on deck - leaks.

-19-

U.S.S. S-26 - Submarine Search and Salvage Operations.
U.S.S. MALLARD, Friday, January 30, 1942.

1534 Over the side.

1535 On the descending line - going down.

1538 Slack the descending line.

1545-30 From diver: Give me slack.

1547 Take me up.

1550 120 ft - On the stage.

1557-30 Diver coming up to 90.

1602 Diver coming up to 80.

1609 Diver coming up to 70.

1617 Diver coming up to 60. Ventilate.

1627 Diver coming up to 50.

1634 Diver on deck.

1700 Preparing diver to go over the side(STOUT,B.E.SF1c.).

1742 Phones OK.

1744 On stage.

1745 On descending line.

1746 150 ft over the side.

1747 200 ft over the side.

1748 300 ft over the side.

1749 Diver on bottom.

1812 Stand by to come up.

1813 Diver starting up.

1816 Diver on stage.

1965 Diver on deck.

-20-

U.S.S. S-26 - Submarine Search and Salvage Operations.
U.S.S. MALLARD, Saturday, January 31, 1942.

U.S.S. MALLARD moored as before. Continuing diving operations. Purpose of diving is to connect blow to starboard side.

1st Diver - SHAHAN, N.C. EMlc.

1200 Preparing to dive.

1226 Over the side.

1229 On the bottom.

1232 Left the bottom.

1235 Diver coming up to 120.

1244 Diver coming up to 90.

1249 Diver coming up to 80.

1256 Diver coming up to 70.

1304 Diver coming up to 60.

1315 Diver coming up to 50.

1446 on board. Decompression on stage at 50 ft.

2nd Diver - WAFFORD, E.C. SFlc.

Purpose of dive to connect blow to starboard side.

1530 Preparing to dive.

1600 Over the side.

1604 On bottom.

1615 Left bottom.

1622 Diver coming up to 130.

1630 Diver coming up to 110.

1632 Diver coming up to 100.

1638 Diver coming up to 90.

1644 Diver coming up to 80.

-21-

U.S.S. S-26 - Submarine Search and Salvage Operations.
U.S.S. MALLARD, Saturday, January 31, 1942.

1654 Diver coming up to 70.

1704 Diver coming up to 60.

1715 Diver coming up to 50.

1720 Surfaced.

-22-

U.S.S. S-26 - Submarine Searching and Salvage Operations.
U.S.S. MALLARD, Sunday, February 1, 1942.

Moored as before over position of the U.S.S. S-26.

Diving and salvage operations continuing.

0800 Preparing to send diver down(GRIFFIN,J.B. CMlc).

0824 Diver over the side - on descending line - going down. Purpose of this dive is to connect blow hose to air salvage fitting.

0828 On the bottom.

0828-30 Give me some slack in life line and air hose.(From diver)

0837 Slack on life line and air hose.(From diver)

1841 Coming up - left bottom.

0845 From diver: Hold that.

1845-30 From diver: More slack on life line and air hose.

0847 From diver: On the stage.

0855 Up to 90.

0859-30 Up to 80.

0906 Up to 70.

0913 Up to 60.

0924 Up to 50.

0927-30 In the chamber.

1000 Preparing diver to go over(EMMET, G.Jr., BMlc.). Purpose of the dive is to connect air blow hose.

1028 Over the side - going down.

1031 On the bottom.

1034 Left the bottom. Short time on the bottom was due to inadequate phone communication, and inability to understand diver necessitated bringing him to the surface.

-23-

U.S.S. S-26 - Submarine Search and Salvage Operations.
U.S.S. MALLARD, Sunday, February 1, 1942.

1038 Diver coming up to 110

1046 Diver coming up to 80

1049 Diver coming up to 70

1053 Diver coming up to 60.

1104 Diver coming up to 50

1115 In the chamber.

1317 Preparing diver to go over (EASON, G.E. GMlc.)

1330 On the stage - over the side.

1330-30 On the descending line - going down.

1331 From diver: Hold it - going down.

1338 From diver: Descending line must be all fouled up with conning tower.

1339 Give me some slack.(from diver)

1339-30 From diver: give me some slack on life line and air hose.

1341 From diver: OK.

1341-30 From diver: Give me more slack.

1342-30 From diver: OK.

1343 From diver: Coming up.

1343-30 From diver: Hold it.

1343-45 From diver: OK - coming up.

1347 Tried to call diver - no answer.

1348 From diver: OK.

1349 From diver: Hold it.

1349-30 From diver: Give me a little slack.

1350 From diver: On the stage.

1358 At 90 ft.

1403 At 80 ft.

-24-

U.S.S. S-26 - Submarine Search and Salvage Operations.
U.S.S. MALLARD, Sunday, February 1, 1942.

1410 At 70 ft.

1418 At 60 ft.

1429 At 50 ft.

1432 On deck - to chamber.

1525 Preparing diver to go over.(FEAGLER, H.H. SF1c.).
Purpose of this dive is to secure new descending line to gun.

1544 Over the side - going down.

1549 On the submarine.

1551 From diver: Take me up.

1555 On the stage. ~~xxxxxx~~.120 Ft.

1603 Diver coming up to 80.

1606 Diver coming up to 70.

1610 Diver coming up to 60.

1621 Diver coming up to 50.

1625 Diver on deck - to the chamber.

1635 Preparing diver to go over the side.(CROCKER,G.F.J. BMlc.,)
The purpose of this dive was to secure descending line to the gun.

1654 Over the side - going down.
1700 On the submarine.
1710 Left the bottom.
1715 Diver coming up - 120 ft.
1723 " " " 90 ft.
1728 " " " 80 ft.
1735 " " " 70 ft
1743 " " " 60 ft.
1754 " " " 50 ft.
1757 Diver on deck - to chamber.

-25-

U.S.S. S-26 - Submarine Search and Salvage Operations.
U.S.S. MALLARD, Monday, February 2, 1942.

Moored as before. Continuing diving operations in connection with the U.S.S. S-26.

0807 Preparing diver to go over(DOMAGALA, W.J. BMlc.,). Purpose of this dive is to connect air salvage hose to starboard side. Two hoses have been lowered to the submarine.

0908 On the stage - over the side.

0908-30 From diver: Going down.

0913 From diver: On the submarine.

0920 From diver: Got hose and ~~connecting~~ shackling it ~~up~~.

0925 From diver: Take in the slack on vent hose.

0926 To diver: Stand by to come up.

0926-30 ~~From~~ To diver: Coming up.

0927-30 From diver: Coming up.

0932 On the stage - 120 ft.

0940 Diver coming up to 90.

0945 Diver coming up to 80.

0952 Diver coming up to 70.

1000 Diver coming up to 60.

1011 Diver coming up to 50.

1014 Diver on deck - in chamber.

1118 Preparing diver to go over(DENISON, H.D. BMlc.) Purpose of this dive is to secure hose.

1125 On the descending line - going down.

1129 On the submarine.

1129-15 From diver: Give me some slack.

-26-

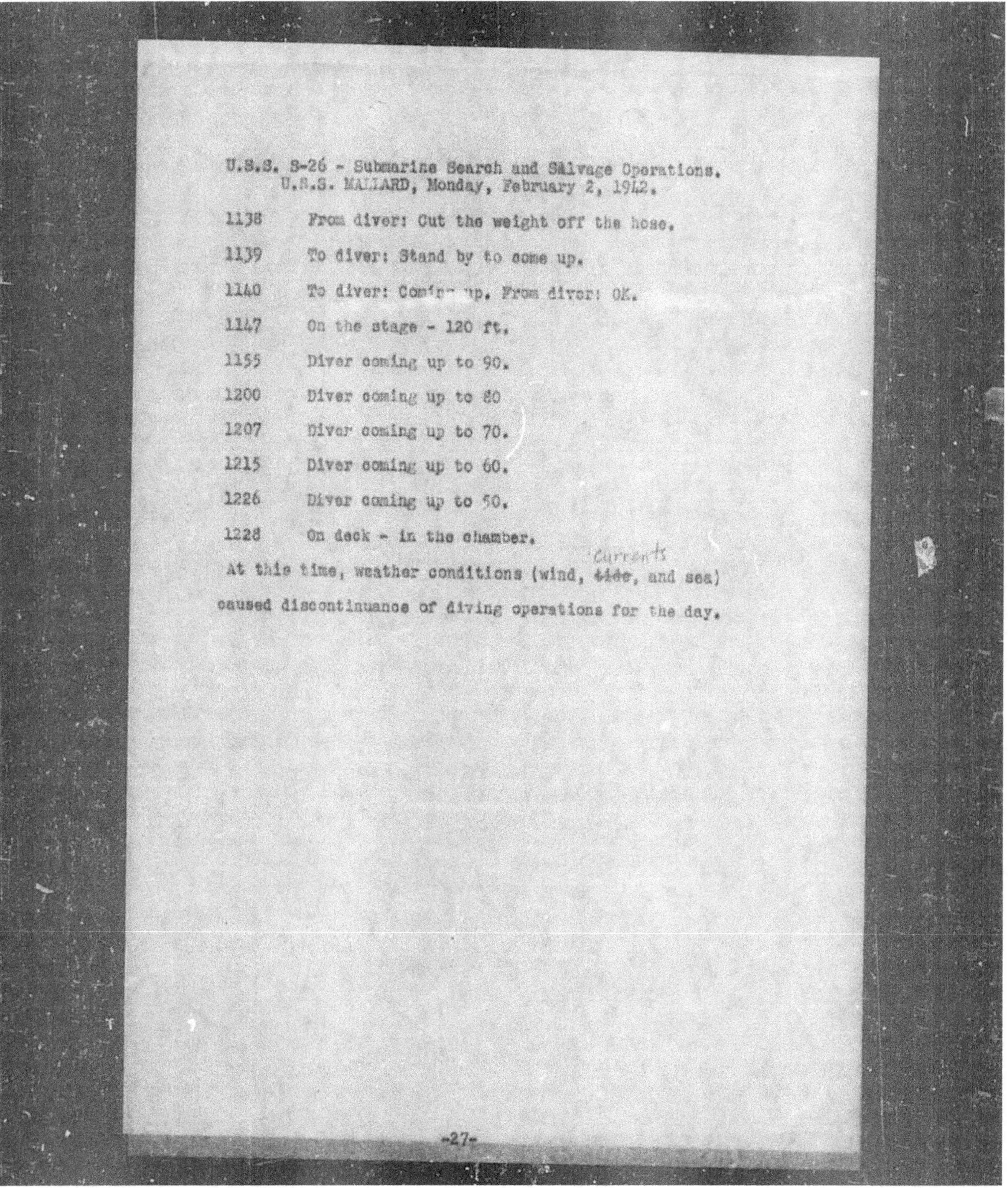

U.S.S. S-26 - Submarine Search and Salvage Operations.
U.S.S. MALLARD, Monday, February 2, 1942.

1138 From diver: Cut the weight off the hose.

1139 To diver: Stand by to come up.

1140 To diver: Coming up. From diver: OK.

1147 On the stage - 120 ft.

1155 Diver coming up to 90.

1200 Diver coming up to 80

1207 Diver coming up to 70.

1215 Diver coming up to 60.

1226 Diver coming up to 50.

1228 On deck - in the chamber.

At this time, weather conditions (wind, ~~tide~~ currents, and sea) caused discontinuance of diving operations for the day.

-27-

U.S.S. S-26 - Submarine Search and Salvage Operations.
U.S.S. MALLARD, Tuesday, February 3, 1942.

NOTE: Strong currents still prevailed and diving operations had to be postponed up to 1100 when operations was continued.

| | |
|---|---|
| 1109 | Preparing diver to go over(AGNESS, R.J., GMlc.). |
| | Purpose of this dive is to inspect new descending line. |
| 1110 | Over the side - going down. |
| 1110-30 | To diver: get on the descending line. |
| 1114 | From diver: Hold it. (On the submarine). |
| 1114-14 | From diver: Give me someslack. |
| 1114-30 | Diver made report on dondition of new descending line. (See statement). |
| 1115-30 | From diver: Lower me away. |
| 1116 | From diver: Hold it. |
| 1116-30 | From diver: Lower me away easy. |
| 1116-45 | From diver: Hold it. |
| 1117 | From diver: Lower me away. |
| 1117-4X30 | From diver: Take me up about 6 foot. |
| 1117-45 | From diver: Hold it. |
| 1117-45 | From diver: Slack me away. |
| 1118-30 | From diver: Take me up. |
| 1119 | From diver: Coming up. |
| 1120 | From diver: Hold it. |
| 1120-15 | From diver: Ok,take me up. |
| 1122 | To diver: Coming up, watch out for the stage. |
| 1122-15 | From diver: Hold it. |
| 1123 | From diver: On the stage - 120. |
| 1131 | Diver coming up to 90. |
| 1136 | Diver coming up to 80. |

-28-

U.S.S. S-26 - Submarine Search and Salvage Operations.
U.S.S. MALLARD, Tuesday, February 3, 1942.

| | |
|---|---|
| 1143 | Diver coming up to 70. |
| 1151 | Diver coming up to 60. |
| 1202 | Diver coming up to 50. |
| 1204 | Diver on deck - in the chamber. |
| 1325 | Preparing diver to go over(SMITH, F.E. CEM). |
| 1327 | On the stage - over the side. |
| 1328 | To diver: Get on the descending line. |
| 1329 | To diver: Get back on the stage. |
| NOTE: | At this time the diver was lowered and raised a couple of feet while the connections on the helmet was tightened. |
| 1330-30 | Diver on the descending line - going down. |
| 1335-30 | From diver: OK on the life line and air hose. |
| 1336 | On the bottom. |
| 1337 | From diver: Ok, take me up. |
| 1337-30 | From diver: Hold that. |
| 1337-45 | From diver: OK, take me up. |
| 1338 | From diver: Hold that. |
| 1338-30 | From diver: Take me up. |
| 1342 | From diver: Hold that. |
| 1342-15 | From diver: On the stage. |
| NOTE: | The purpose of this dive was to establish the descending line and hook up the hose. |
| 1344 | From diver: Give me a little slack on life line and air hose. |
| 1350 | Diver coming up to 90. |

-29-

U.S.S. S-26 - Submarine Search and Salvage Operations.
U.S.S. MALLARD, Tuesday, February 3, 1942.

1355 Diver coming up to 80.

1402 Diver coming up to 70.

1410 Diver coming up to 60.

1421 Diver coming up to 50.

1423 Diver on deck - in chamber.

-30-

DIVING OPERATIONS

Wednesday, 28 January, 1942.

STATEMENT OF DENISON, H.D. BMlc.,

As I went down the descending line the angle of the line made it necessary for me to pull myself down. My arms became tired and I ask the topside to take me up. Otherwise I felt OK.

Thursday, 29 January, 1942.

STATEMENT OF AGNESS, R.J. GMlc.,

Went down to within about thirty feet of the submarine when the angle of the descending line was such that I was forced to pull myself the remaining distance to the boat. Landed on the superstructure six feet forward of the stern planes. Went aft to stern planes until I could see screws. Slid over the side to work myself forward. Went underneath the submarine to look at bottom of ship. Kicked hull three times and listened. Went up on the turn of the bilge and worked forward - kicked again - put helmet against hull and listened - was recalled to descending line and went up.

DIVING OPERATIONS(Contd)

Friday, 30 January 1942.

STATEMENT OF SMITH, F.E. CBM., (Dive #1.)

Landed on submarine about thirty feet aft of the conning tower on starboard side. Took descending line forward and secured it to seat on the starboard side of the gun. Inspected hatch leading to C.?.C. and found it closed. Returned to descending line and came to surface. Visibility was about eight feet. Telephone worked OK but communication was inadequate. (SMITH later stated he meant the "conning tower hatch" and that he meant he had difficulty in getting communications through).

STATEMENT OF STOUT, D.E. SFlc., (Dive #2)

I landed on the breach of the gun, unshackled the hose from the descending line and carried it aft on the starboard side, and secured it to the life line above the deck cleat. I spent the rest of my time looking for deck fittings for air salvage connections but was unable to find any due to darkness. The purpose of this dive was to prepare for connecting blow hose.

DIVING OPERATIONS(Contd)

Saturday, 31 January, 1942.

STATEMENT OF SHAHAN, N.G. EMlc.,(Dive #1).

I went down to connect hose to salvage fitting. Descending line was curved with the tide and I had to pull myself aboard. Tide was too strong and I was too tired to complete the job. I ask to be brought up.

STATEMENT OF WAFFORD, E.C. SFlc., (Dive #2).

I landed on the starboard wing of the conning tower where frame for antenna wire projects outboard. The descending line led from forward underneath this frame and from there almost straight up. After or while landing on submarine there was enough slack in my life line and air hose to get a loop over the outboard end of antenna frame which I had trouble clearing. I had trouble using my right hand due to air in glove and after clearing loop I was pretty tired. I asked the tope side how long I had been down and was told ten minutes. I then decided that there was not time enough left to accomplish any more and did not go down on deck. After starting up, when about 40 or 50 feet.off the bottom, I discovered that there was a complete turn around the descending line of my air hose which tended to lock around descending line upon being pulled from topside. After about four attempts and asking for and getting slack from the topside I succeeded in getting enough slack below me to hold the bight off the life line and hose with my left foot thereby keeping the strain off the descending line, I was then pulled up to the stage.

DIVING OPERATIONS(Contd)

Sunday, 1 February, 1942.

STATEMENT OF GRIFFIN, J.B. CMlc., (Dive #1).

Upon reaching the bottom I found the starboard seat of the gun to which the descending line was secured to be carried away. I landed outboard of the submarine, pulled myself up on deck, and proceeded to resecure the descending line, paying particular attention that it was clear of all obstacles that might be in the way of future dives. I secured the descending line to the starboard life line stanchion abreast of the conning tower. I cleared the blow hose as well as I could and then went aft on starboard fairwater to find the air salvage connection. I found the fitting alright but had difficultly trying to loosen the fitting as I could not get a good purchase on wrench. My left arm was very tired from heaving on the blow hose and descending line. So I though it best to start back to my descending line before tiring too much. I would say that visibility was about 12 feet. The submarine is on an even keel as near as I could judge. One section of the life line on the starboard side just forward of fairwater is carried away.

DIVING OPERATIONS(Contd)

Sunday, 1 February, 1942.

STATEMENT OF EMMET, C. BM1c., (Dive #2).

I landed on deck and moved aft to the air salvage fitting. Picked up the wrench and unscrewed the cap and took it completely off and laid it on the deck alongside of me. At that time they started taking me up. This was due to inadequate communication over the batteryless telephones.

STATEMENT OF EASON, G.E. GM1c., (Dive #3).

I landed on the conning tower and worked my way down on to the deck. [illegible] gun seat is hanging on the descending line between the conning tower and the life line. The submarine seemed to be very level. My arms were very tired from the descent and I ask tocome up. Communication was very poor. Visibility appeared to be between 5 and 8 feet. I saw a brass name plate on the conning tower but didn't notice what was on it. (EASON later stated that he meant he landed on the "bridge").

STATEMENT OF FEAGLER, H.H. SF1c., (Dive #4).

Reached the submarine and was supposed to secure new descending line. New descending line was dropped in the conning tower. I lifted the weight out of the conning tower and dropped it to the deck of the submarine. It was clear of everything. I was too tired to get down on deck so I ask to come up. Visibility was between 8 and 10 feet when looking at bright objects. The blackness of the boat could not be distinquished except at very close range. (FEAGLER later stated that he meant the "bridge" instead of the "conning tower".)

DIVING OPERATIONS(Contd)

Sunday, 1 February, 1942.

STATEMENT OF CROCKER, C.F.J., BMlc.(Dive #5).

I landed on fair water and sat down to rest. Then I got hold of the new descending line with the 9 thread attached to it and cut the 9 thread loose and started down the port side. The 9 thread got caught and the new descending line slipped right through my hand. I couldn't squeeze enough to hold it and it went overboard with the weight that was attached to it. I came back up on the cigarette deck and went over to the starboard side and looked at the old descending line and looked at the hose. They were secured. I was told to stand by to come up. Telephone communication was very poor. Visibility was about 4 feet. The submarine appeared to be on a even keel. Nothing unusual about it. ( CROCKER later described the "fair-water" as the upper after part of the periscope shears).

DIVING OPERATIONS(Contd).
Monday, February 2, 1942.

STATEMENT OF DOMAGALA, W.J. BMlc(Dive #1).

I didn't feel so much current. I landed on the starboard side outboard of the rail. The gun seat is attached to the descending line and is hanging over the side. I swung myself in on deck and rested awhile. The weight on the vent hose landed in between the descending line and the blow hose that crossed the descending line. I could not get the vent hose clear. I secured the stop on the vent hose to the rail and then cut the line between the shackle on the descending line and the weight on the vent hose. This left the vent hose hanging overboard with the weight attached, in between the blow hose and the descending line. Visibility is between 8 and 9 feet. Nothing unusual was encountered. The cap was off the blow to the CCC. Communications over the RCA telephone was very good.

STATEMENT OF DENISON, H.D., BMlc (Dive #2).

I landed on the ~~conning tower~~ bridge and walked down the ladder to the deck. I pulled the vent hose inboard and cut the weight off, and left the hose secured to the rail. I spent the rest of the time looking for the connection. I didn't find it. I was then told to stand by to come up. I had some difficulty coming up because the descending line was fouled in the outrigging of the conning tower. Visibility was about 5 to 8 feet. Communications was very good.

NOTE: Strong current conditions precluded further diving operations for today.

DIVING OPERATIONS(Contd).
Tuesday, February 3, 1942.

STATEMENT OF AGNESS, R.J. GMlc., (DIVE #1).

I landed on the port antenna astride the grapnel on the descending line, forward of the conning tower. Got slack on descending line and tried to lower myself by using the blow hose. I slid down the hose intending to land on deck but the tide was so great that I landed on the bottom over the port side. I tried to pull myself back up to the rail but the tide was too strong. Then I pulled myself up to the antenna and tried to drop on deck but didn't succeed. I went over the side again. This time I pulled myself back up to the antenna, got hold of the descending line and was too tired to continue further operations. So I ask to come up. The purpose of my dive was to establish the location and, if possible, secure the descending line. I was unable to secure it so I left it on the Antenna were the grapnel is hooked. The tide was especially strong. Visibility was about 4 feet. Nothing unusual occured. The submarine didn't seem to have shifted. Communications were very good.

STATEMENT OF SMITH, F.R. CRM(Dive #2).

I reached a point to within eight feet of where the grapnel hook on the descending line was hooked to the submarine antenna. From this point I could see that the two hoses, we have down, were leading under the grapnel chain with about 120° up angle. The last 50 ft of the descent had been extremely difficult, because of both the tide pull on the life line and air hose and the horizontal angle of the descending line, about the 50 or 60 feet seemed to be on a level with where the grapnel was hooked.

DIVING OPERATIONS(Contd).
Tuesday, February 3, 1942.

STATEMENT OF SMITH, F.E. CBM(Contd).

I was barely able to hold on to the descending line and decided not to go any farther so asked to be pulled up.

The tide at the 120, 90, 80 and 70 foot decompression stops was running at about seven knots. At the 60 foot level it seemed to slow considerable and the water was much clearer. Visibility at the bottom was between 8 and 10 ft. Communications were very good.

Sunday, 25 Jan (Daylight)

79-25 79-20 08-20 79-15

Woodcock planted buoy + dragged area 08-15

S/M's search

Sampson + Mallard + 3 small boats conducted sound, magnetic drag, + sensitive hydrophone search

Elda dragging

Barry planted buoy

S/M's search

Sampson search

Slick

Sampson joined + commenced sound search in this vicinity. Sampson + Barry investigated oil slicks for 2 hours. Other vessels searching in vicinity of buoys

Picked up Message Buoy

Woodcock joined up

Received various contact reports + objects sighted – no results.

Barry

S-21 S-29 Eldo S-44

Tuna Clipper

08-16

Plane searched entire area

To oil slicks

Sunday, 25 Jan. Daylight

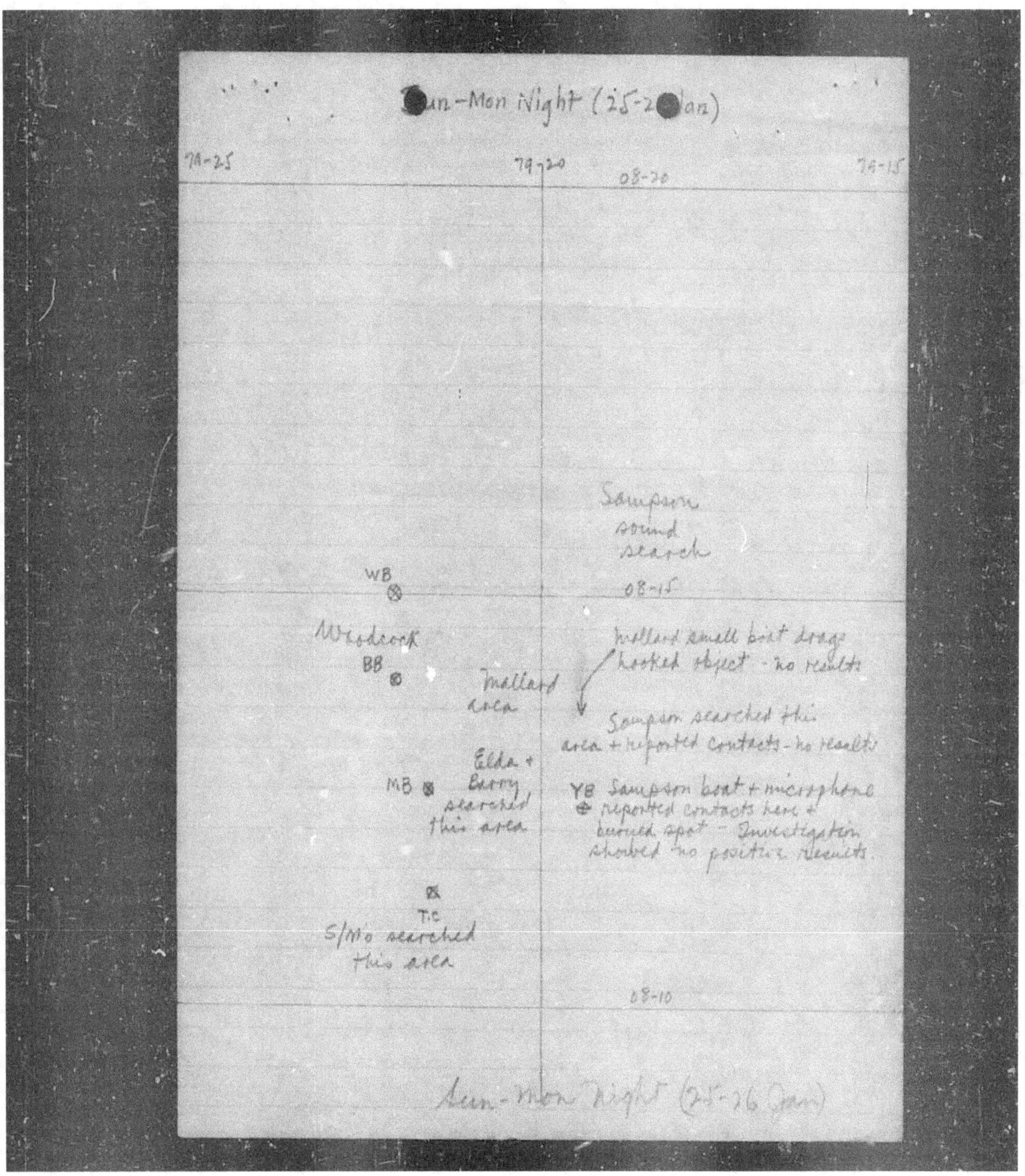
79-25
79-20
08-20
79-15
Sampson
sound
search
WB
08-15
Woodcock
BB
Mallard small boat drags
hooked object - no results
Mallard
area
Sampson searched this
area + reported contacts - no results
Elda +
Barry
searched
this area
MB
YB Sampson boat + microphone
reported contacts here +
buoyed spot - Investigation
showed no positive results.
T.C
S/Mo searched
this area
08-10
Sun-Mon Night (25-26 Jan)

Monday Daylight (26 Jan)

79-25
79-20
08-20
79-15

Sampson

also using small boats with magnetic sweeps + microphone

Favorite along this latitude

WB

08-15

E.P

Mallard Woodcock magnetic + Favorite dragging

Barry search

BB

Eelda search

MB

Same search here with Sampson

YB

Sampson search

S/Ms search

T.B

Barry investigated previous location of oil slicks - no results

08-10

Plane searched entire area Mon. Daylight (26 Jan)

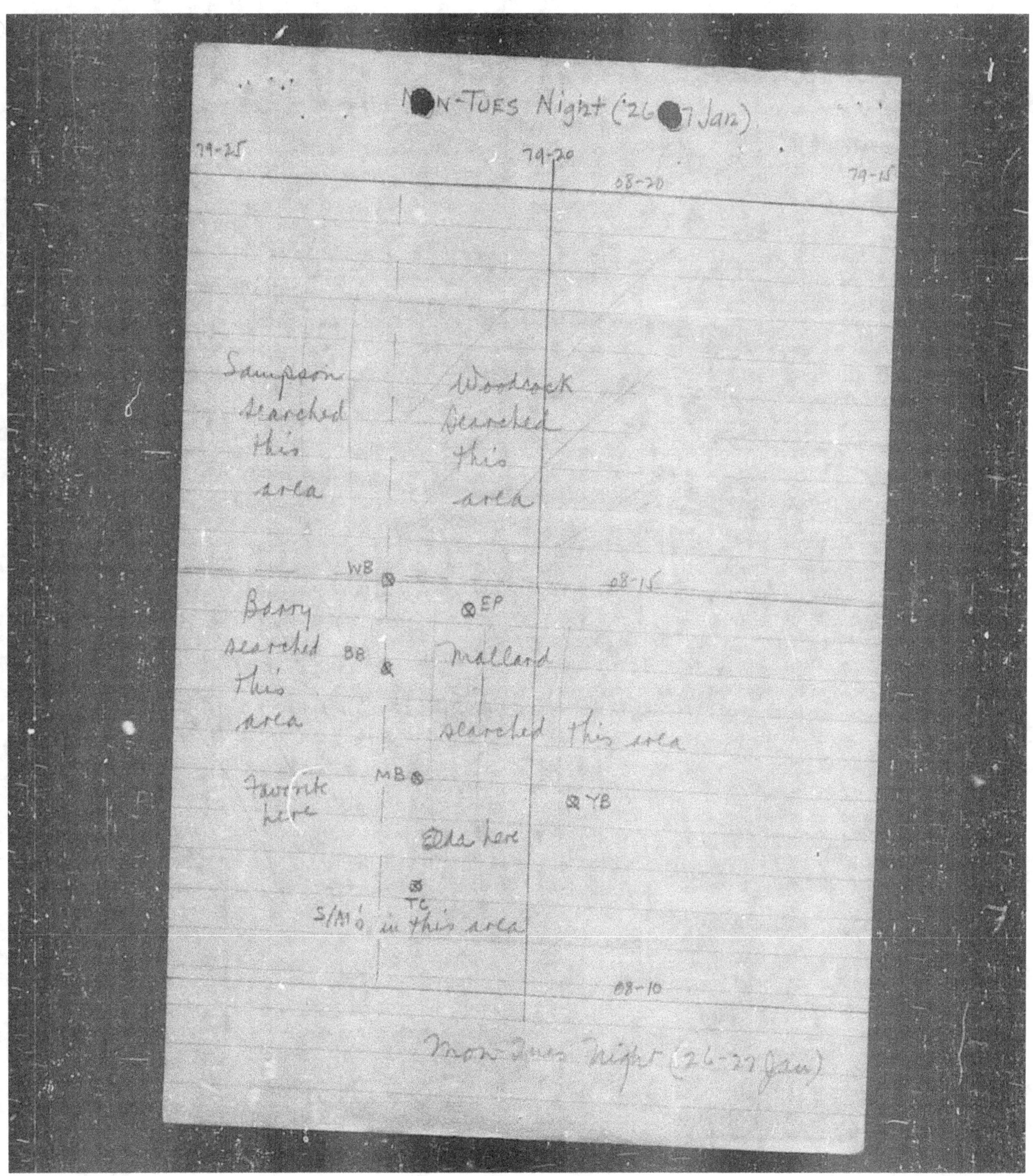
MON-TUES Night (26-27 Jan)
79-25
79-20
08-20
79-15
Sampson searched this area
Woodcock searched this area
WB
08-15
EP
Barry searched this area
BB
Mallard
searched this area
MB
Favorite here
YB
Ida here
TC
S/M's in this area
08-10
Mon-Tues Night (26-27 Jan)

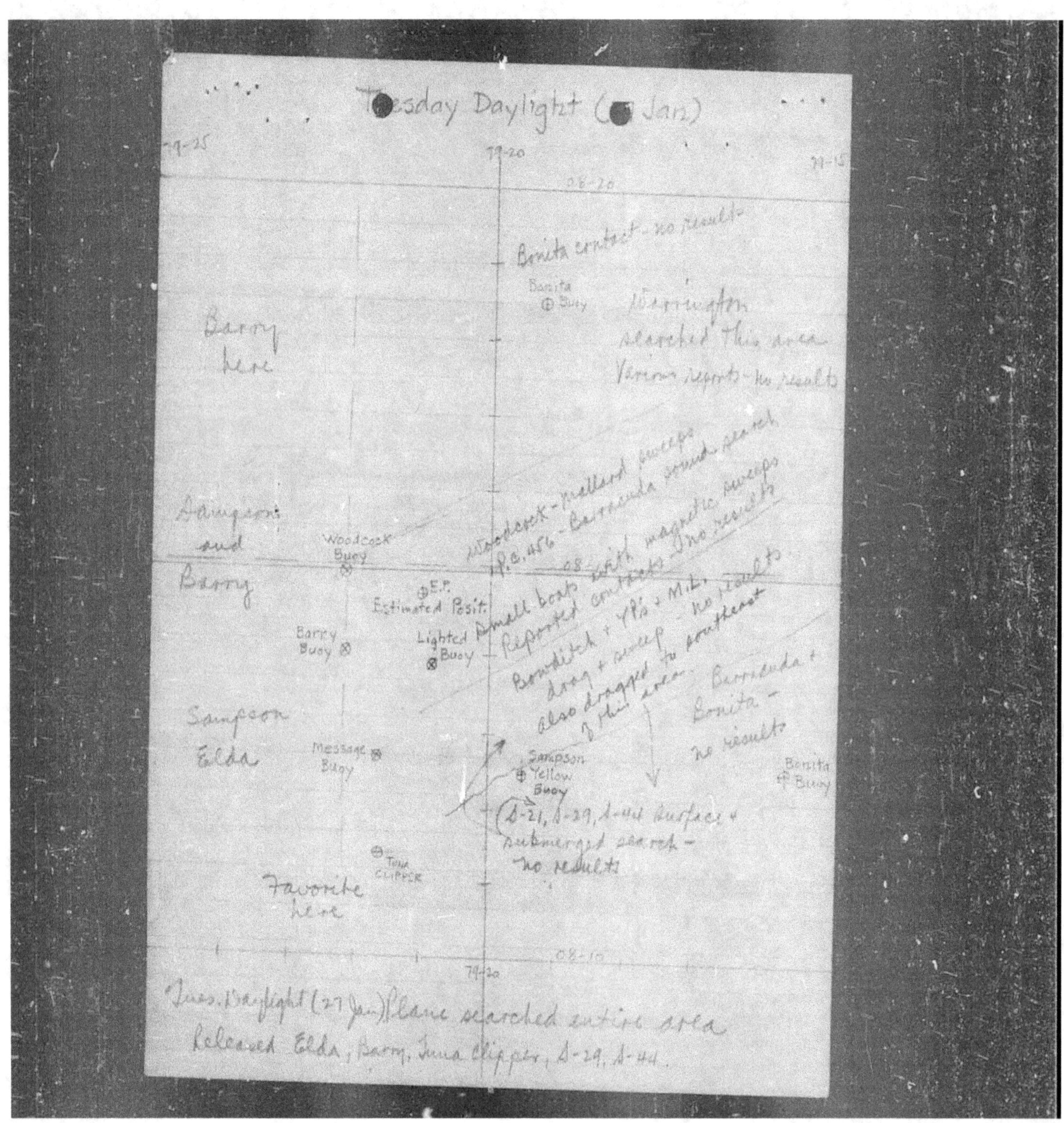
esday Daylight ( Jan)
79-25
79-20
79-15
08-20
Bonita contact - no results
Bonita Buoy
Herrington searched this area
Various reports - no results
Barry here
Woodcock - pollard sweeps
P.C. 456 - Barracuda sound search
Small boats with magnetic sweeps
Reported contacts - no results
Sampson and Barry
Woodcock Buoy
08
E.P. Estimated Posit.
Barry Buoy
Lighted Buoy
Bowditch + YP's + M.L. drag + sweep - no results
also dragged to southeast of this area
Barracuda + Bonita - no results
Sampson Elda
Message Buoy
Sampson Yellow Buoy
Bonita Buoy
S-21, S-29, S-44 surface + submerged search - no results
Tuna Clipper
Favorite here
08-10
79-20
Tues. Daylight (27 Jan) Plane searched entire area
Released Elda, Barry, Tuna Clipper, S-29, S-44.

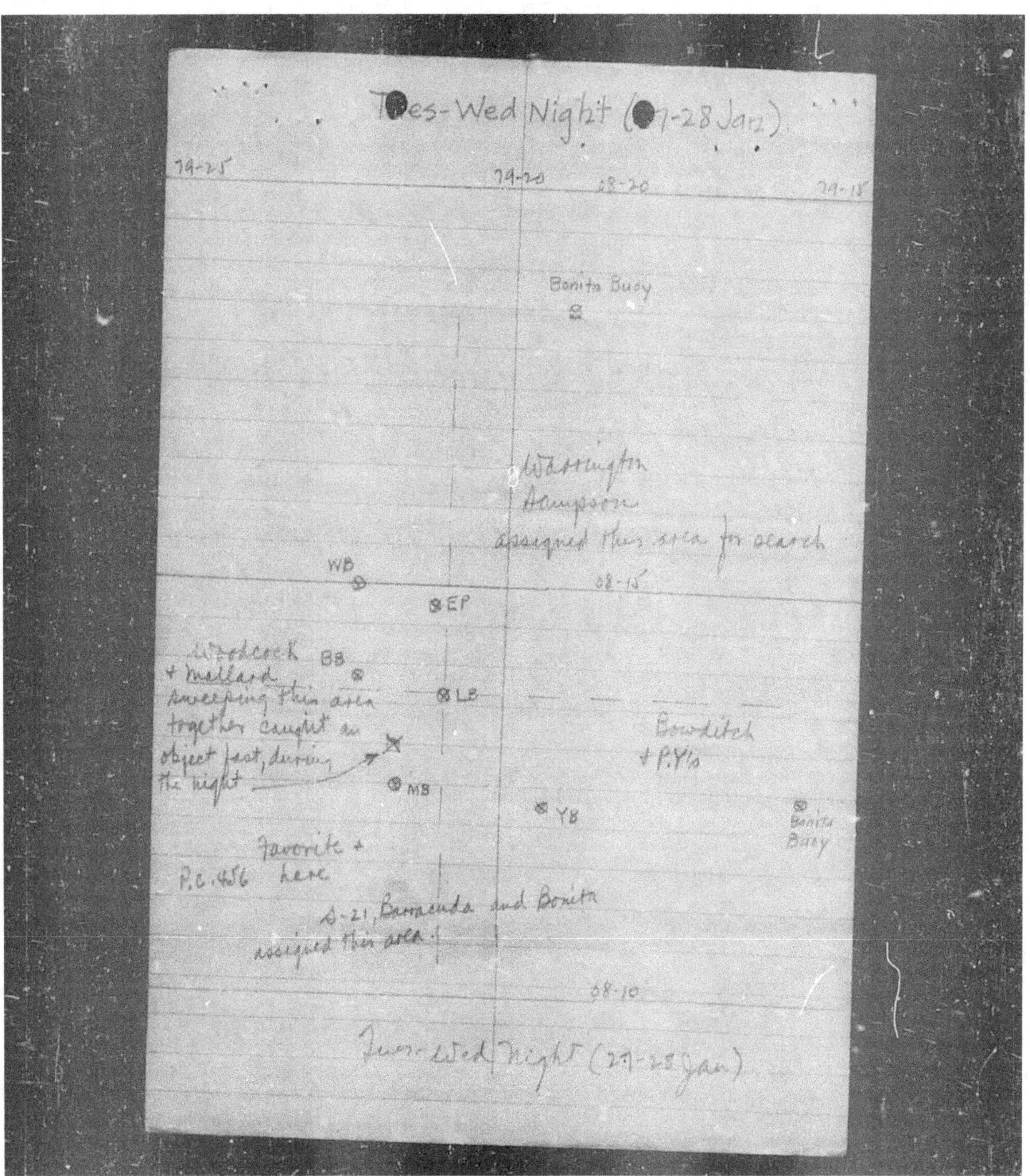
Tues-Wed Night (27-28 Jan)
79-25
79-20
08-20
79-15
Bonita Buoy
Washington
Sampson
assigned this area for search
WB
08-15
EP
Woodcock
+ Mallard
sweeping this area
together caught an
object fast, during
the night
BB
LB
MB
Bowditch
+ P.Y's
YB
Bonita
Buoy
Favorite +
P.C. 456 here
S-21, Barracuda and Bonita
assigned this area
08-10
Tues-Wed Night (27-28 Jan)

Wed. Daylight (28 Jan)

79-25 79-20 08-20 79-15

Bonita Buoy

Warrington and Sampson

WB

08-15

EP

BB

LB

Woodcock + Mallard maneuvered around this spot until Mallard moored in late afternoon

MB

(2-21, Barracuda, Bonita) A/M's in this area

YB

Bonita Buoy

Bowditch and P.Y's.

Favorite + P.C. 456

08-10

Plane searched entire area Wed. Daylight (28 Jan)

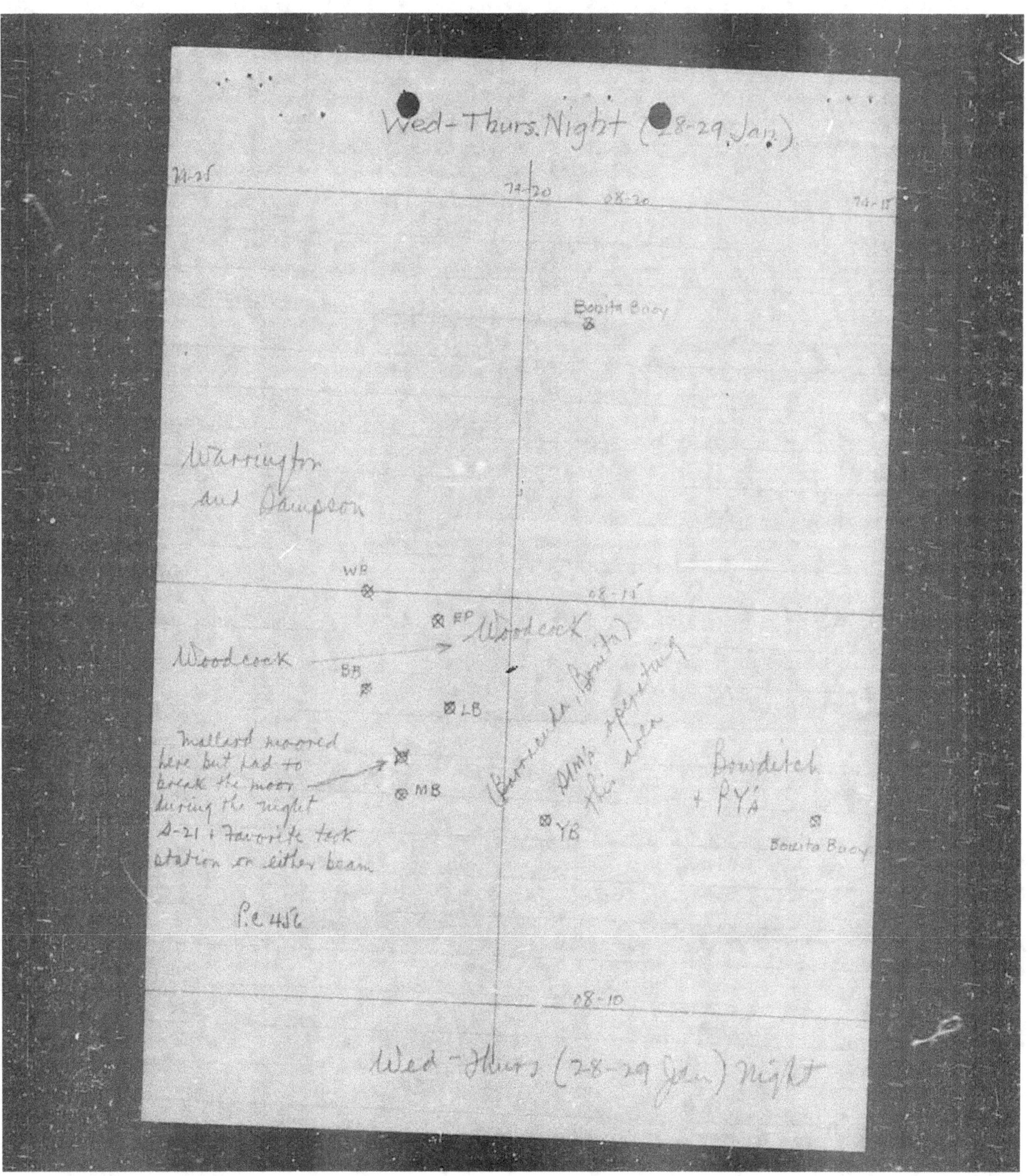

Wed-Thurs. Night (28-29 Jan.)
74-25
74-20
08-20
74-15
Bonita Buoy
Warrington and Sampson
WB
08-15
EP
Woodcock
Woodcock
BB
LB
(Barracuda, Bonita)
DM's operating this area
Mallard moored here but had to break the moor during the night S-21 & Favorite took station on either beam
MB
YB
Bowditch & PY's
Bonita Buoy
P.C. 456
08-10
Wed-Thurs (28-29 Jan) Night

Thurs. Daylight (29 Jan).

79-25 79-20 08-20 79-15

Bonita Buoy

Warrington and Sampson

WB

08-15

EP

BB

Woodcock assisting

LB

Barracuda + Bonita here

Mallard maneuvered around the spot + moored. Diver went down + located S/M.

MB

Bowditch + P.Y.'s here

YB

Bonita Buoy

Favorite + S-21 standing by

P.C. 456

08-10

Plane searched entire area Thurs. Daylight (29 Jan).

CONFIDENTIAL

USS Beaver-2-8-41-6M

CSS 5 L11-1 203
CSD 51
CSD 52
CSD 53 File No.

Received from Comsubdiv-51 on February 10 1942

File No. of February 3 1942

Subject Loss of U.S.S. S-26 (Search operations, etc)

Enc. 6

| | | SYMBOL | INITIALS | SYMBOLS |
|---|---|---|---|---|
| 00 | Sqdn. Commander | 2 | | A For Information |
| 01 | C. S. D. 51 | | | B Take Appropriate Action |
| 02 | C. S. D. 53 | | | C For Recommendation |
| 03 | C. S. D. 52 | 2 | | D Prepare Draft Reply |
| 90 | Gunnery | 2 | | E Retain Copy, if desired |
| 20 | Communications | 2 | | F Consult Sqdn. Comdr. |
| 70 | Engineer | 2 | | K Distribute to Squadron |
| 71 | Asst. Material | | | |
| 60 | Personnel | | | |
| | Chief Yeoman | | | |

ACTION Required by (Date)

Write Letter to
Endorsement

Via Copies to

forwarded
approval recommended
for compliance
for information
approved
for guidance
concurring in end
for distribution
returned

REMARKS:

05 send to Consultant for his info & return — C

L11-1

CONFIDENTIAL

Finished, File (initials)

FB51/A16

Serial 037

SUBMARINE DIVISION FIFTY-ONE
U. S. S. S-1, Flagship
c/o Postmaster, Morgan Annex,
New York, New York,
February 19, 1942.

DECLASSIFIED - OPNAV INST 5500.30
BY [illegible] DATE 11-1-60

From: The Commander Submarine Division Fifty-One.
To : The Chief of Naval Operations.
The Commander in Chief, Atlantic Fleet.
The Commander Submarines, Atlantic Fleet.

Subject: Report of War Patrols.

Reference: (a) Comsublant ltr. No. 14-41, File A6-5(1979) of December 15, 1941.

Enclosures: (A) Report of War Patrol - U.S.S. S-21.
(B) Report of War Patrol - U.S.S. S-29.

1. In accordance with reference (a) Enclosures (A) and (B) are forwarded herewith.

2. The patrols of these two vessels were interrupted on the occasion of the escort vessel (USS Elda, PC 460) ramming and sinking the S-26. The S-21 and S-29 were used as part of the searching group, while the S-21 was also used as sample ship for the divers in attempts at rescue.

3. The patrol was completed without enemy contact. In connection with this it is recommended that wherever practicable friendly merchantmen be routed outside of submarine patrol areas. In such case, the submarine can then generally assume that any merchantmen sighted are fair game. The time required by a submarine to definitely determine the status of a merchantman would almost always nullify chances for attack.

4. I believe that our own and Allied communication forces should continue working together to simplify the present confusing system of recognition and emergency identification signals. As a constructive suggestion I believe that a one or two letter system changing, say, every day would remove some of the complexity in our system.

C. F. ERCK.

FEB 23 1942

Copy to: CSS 5.
Comsuboffshopacpanseafrontfor.
S-21
S-29

44372

40127

U.S. S. S-21

February 14, 1942.

From: The Commanding Officer.
To : The Commander Submarine Division Fifty-One.

Subject: Report of Period at sea from January 24, 1942 to February 7, 1942.

1. In accordance with Commander Submarines Offshore Patrol Pacific mailgram 200800 of January this vessel proceeded on war patrol in Pacific waters off Panama on January 24, 1942. Transit of the canal was effected on January 24, joined the escort vessel, USS Elda, off the station ship at the entrance to Balboa and proceeded to point SA in company with escort vessel and S-26, S-29, and S-44. A trim dive was made in the early evening of January 24, 1942.

2. The escort left the formation at 2210 January 24, having signaled that she was at a point 14 miles west of San Jose light. At 2230 course was changed to 204° for point SB. At 2335 a signal was received from the escort saying that she had struck and sunk the S-26.

3. Course was immediately changed to head for the ELDA and the Commander Submarine Squadron Three notified by radio. Eight lookouts were placed on watch and a careful lookout maintained during the night for any survivors or signs of wreckage. The Commander Submarine Squadron Three arrived early the next morning, January 25, and took charge of the search operations. This vessel was retained to continue the search for the S-26 and then to serve as a guide for the divers while engaged in salvage operations, for the next two weeks.

4. SUMMARY OF EVENTS:

Jan 24. 1737 - Falling in with escort off station ship at Balboa.
2210 - Escort left the formation having reached the approximate location of point SA.
2219 - Necessary to change course to the left to avoid the escort.
2230 - Changed course to 204°.
2235 - Received a signal from the escort saying that she had struck and sunk the S-26. Immediately changed course and headed for the escort.
2250 - Reached escort, slowed down and spent remainder of night looking for survivors or wreckage.

-1-

2

DECLASSIFIED U.S.S. S-21

Subject: Report of Period at Sea from January 24, 1942 to February 7, 1942.

- - - - - - - - - - - - - - - - - - - - - - - - - - - - - - - - - - - -

4. SUMMARY OF EVENTS(Contd).

Jan 25. 0620 - Commander Submarine Squadron Three reached scene in DD 248. At daylight commenced a general search of area, working to the North, looking for any traces of the S-26.

1120 - Directed by Comsubron 3 to search, with S-29 and S-44, a four mile square area North of present position (Lat.8-15 N and Long. 79-24 W), and that a message from the S-26 had been picked up.

1746 - Took night station as directed by Comsubron 3.

Jan 26. 0648 - Commenced search of area North of Tuna Clipper on East-West courses in company with S-29 and S-44. At about five minute intervals would stop to listen through hull for any tapping.

1820 - Took night station.

Jan 27. 0834 - Commenced listening search, with S-29 and S-44, in vicinity of yellow buoy (about a mile and a half Northeast of Tuna Clipper).

1200 - Requested and obtained permission to dive South of yellow buoy on course 270° to try and listen at 100'.

1325 - Submerged.

1425 - Surfaced, no results.

1446 - Received a message that S-29 and S-44 were released from present duty.

1915 - Took night station between BONITA and BARRACUDA.

Jan 28. ---- - Conducted a general search in vicinity of original anchorage of Tuna Clipper.

1806 - Took night station 1500 yards East of MALLARD, now anchored.

Jan 29. --- - At daylight somewhat South of MALLARD, found two pronounced oil slicks and BARRACUDA investigated this area with sound on instructions from Comsubron 3.

1420 - Intercepted a message saying that S-26 had been located.

Feb 6. ---- - At sunset set "ALERT" on orders from Comsubron 3.

Feb 7. 1153 - Submerged astern of MALLARD during funeral services for S-26 to float wreath.

1157 - Surfaced and half masted colors.

1210 - Reported to Comsubdiv 31 that S-21 had been released.

-2-

3

U. S. S. S-21

DECLASSIFIED

Subject: Report of Period at sea from January 24, 1942 to February 7, 1942.

- - - - - - - - - - - - - - - - - - - - - - - - - - - - - - - - - -

4. SUMMARY OF EVENTS(Contd).

Feb 7(Contd)
1516 - Ahead on both engines proceeding to Balboa in accordance with instructions.
1840 - Off station ship, pilot came on board.
1947 - Moored starboard side to USS GOLDSBOROUGH at Pier 18 G. Pilot left the ship.

Feb 8. 0758 - Pilot came on board (Mr. Kilcorse).
0802 - Underway.
1600 - Transit completed, pilot left the ship off Cristobal Mole.
1628 - Moored starboard side to North side Pier 1, Submarine Base, Coco Solo, C.Z.

5. Torpedoes were kept in the ready condition at all times. No torpedoes were found that had excessive loss of air.

6. The general weather conditions during the two weeks off the MALLARD in the Gulf of Panama were ideal. A strong current was experienced at irregular times, which made station keeping off the MALLARD difficult.

7. The ship was quite habitable although the temperature of the after battery went up because the engines were not run continuously.

8. The morale of the crew was good. They were kept busy by daily ship drills and school of the ship. During week day mornings submerged exercises were held about two miles South of the MALLARD. The gun's crew was exercised using the MALLARD as a target and all new seamen and firemen received instruction in pointing and training. All men who had not fired the pistal within the past year received instruction and fired several clips of ammunition. Semaphore and blinker drill were held for the deck force.

9. In view of the loss of the S-26 it is strongly recommended that the escort have officers on board who are acquainted with submarines. If this cannot be done it is recommended, when submarines are to be escorted at night, that a submarine officer, preferably a commanding officer or a division commander be on board the escort to advise the commanding officer of submarine limitations. This would be similar to having a submarine commanding officer, or division commander, on board the target while conducting torpedo firing rehearsals.

J.A. BOLE, JR.

LOGISTIC DATA

U.S.S. S-21

| DATE | Jan 24 | Jan 25 | Jan 26 | Jan 27 | Jan 28 | Jan 29 | Jan30 | Jan31 |
|---|---|---|---|---|---|---|---|---|
| Fuel Used | 371 | 758 | 407 | 484 | 358 | 253 | 140 | 298 |
| Fuel on hand 2400 | 25,327 | 24,569 | 24,162 | 23,678 | 23,320 | 23,180 | 23,040 | 22,742 |
| Lub Used. | 62 | 40 | 40 | 40 | 15 | 16 | 14 | 16 |
| Lub on hand 2400 | 2062 | 2022 | 1982 | 1942 | 1927 | 1911 | 1897 | 1881 |
| Fresh Water used | 60 | 160 | 100 | 167 | 99 | 115 | 153 | 109 |
| Water Distilled. | - | - | - | 140 | 186 | 65 | 80 | 182 |
| Water on hand 2400 | 960 | 800 | 700 | 673 | 760 | 710 | 637 | 710 |
| Hours C&R A.C. Run. | - | - | - | (1) 2.0 | - | (1) 0.4 | - | (1) 1.1 |
| Battery Water used | - | - | - | - | - | - | - | - |
| Battery Water on hand 2400 | 870 | 870 | 870 | 870 | 870 | 870 | 870 | 870 |
| Provisions on hand (Fresh) | 5 | 4 | 3 | 2 | 1 | - | - | - |
| (Days)(Dry) | 30 | 29 | 28 | 27 | 26 | 25 | 24 | 23 |

5

U.S.S. S-21

LOGISTIC DATA

| DATE | Feb 1 | Feb 2 | Feb 3 | Feb 4 | Feb 5 | Feb 6 | Feb 7 | Feb 8 |
|---|---|---|---|---|---|---|---|---|
| Fuel Used | 60 | 107 | 335 | 158 | 232 | 122 | 465 | 166 |
| Fuel on hand 2400 | 22,682 | 22,575 | 22,240 | 22,082 | 21,850 | 21,728 | 21,263 | 21,097 |
| Lub Used. | 15 | 16 | 35 | 16 | 25 | 22 | 35 | 22 |
| Lub on hand 2400 | 1866 | 1850 | 1815 | 1799 | 1774 | 1752 | 1717 | 1695 |
| Fresh Water used | 109 | 105 | 91 | 113 | 98 | 174 | 230 | - |
| Water Distilled. | - | - | 218 | - | 138 | 14 | 140 | - |
| Water on hand 2400 | 601 | 496 | 623 | 510 | 550 | 390 | 300 | - |
| Hours C&R A.C. Run. | - | - | - | - | (1) 1.2 | - | - | - |
| Battery Water used | - | - | - | - | - | - | - | - |
| Battery Water on hand 2400 | 870 | 870 | 870 | 870 | 870 | 870 | 870 | 870 |
| Provisions on hand (Fresh) | - | - | - | - | - | - | - | - |
| (Days)(Dry) | 22 | 21 | 20 | 19 | 18 | 17 | 16 | 15 |

6

SS134/A16
Serial (05)
C [DECLASSIFIED] T A L

U.S.S. S-29
c/o Postmaster
New York, N.Y.
February 13, 1942

From: The Commanding Officer.
To : The Commander Submarine Division Fifty-One.

Subject: Report of War Patrol - Period January 24 to February 9, 1942.

1. In accordance with Comsubron Three Operation Plan No. 40-41 and Commander Submarines Offshore Patrol Pacific, secret mailgram 200800 of January, 1942, this vessel proceeded on war patrol in Pacific waters off Panama on January 24, 1942, joined escort vessel, U.S.S. ELDA near Pacific entrance to canal at 1754 and proceeded to point "A" on course 169°T in company with escort vessel and U.S.S. S-21, S-26 and S-44. Pilot released at 1603 in Balboa Harbor. Canal was cleared at 1745. At 1830 made trim dive, surfaced and rejoined escort vessel at 1925.

2. At 2220, escort vessel reversed course to leave formation, and at 2225 passed abeam to starboard at about 1500 yards distance. At approximately 2229, escort vessel appeared to back down very suddenly in attempt to avoid collision with U.S.S. S-26, whose position was about three points on the starboard quarter at about 2500 yards distance. At 2233 escort vessel sent SOS by searchlight. At 2235 this vessel changed course to the left and headed for escort vessel at full speed on both engines, the Captain taking conn. At 2243 arrived in vicinity of escort vessel and began search of surface with searchlight for survivors or wreckage of U.S.S. S-26. Because of depth of water of 51 fathoms by chart soundings, vessel was unable to anchor. At 2315 sighted what was believed to be a piece of white cork of about four inches square. At 2330 sighted white life jacket in water, which was thought to have been dropped by crew of escort vessel's boats which were in water. Conducted visual and sound search for S-26 until released by Commander Submarine Squadron Three at 1440 January 27, 1942, at which time instructions were requested and received by dispatch from Commander Submarines, Offshore Patrol, Pacific.

3. At 1800, January 27, 1942 proceeded to point "B" in company with S-44 on course 202° T. At 0345, January 28, 1942 passed point "Sail B", changed course, astern of S-44, to 270° T, proceeding to point "Sail C". At 1515, changed course to 268° T, proceeding independently to patrol area. At 1246 January 31, 1942 message was received changing

-1-

SS134/A16
Serial (05)
C [illegible] I A L
DECLASSIFIED

U.S.S. S-29
c/o Postmaster
New York, N.Y.
February 13, 1942

Subject: Report of War Patrol - Period January 24, to February 9, 1942.

3.(Contd)

patrol station, and at 1306, changed course to 225°T to head for newly assigned station.

4. Arrived on patrol station, latitude 5° N, longitude 93° W at 0230 February 1, 1942, and commenced patrol, zig-zagging, base course 270° T, speed 5 during daylight, and on base course 090° T during darkness arranging courses and speeds during late night run to arrive on station at 0700 each day.

5. Summary of events:

| | | |
|---|---|---|
| 24 Jan | 2150 | Sighted ship bearing 172° T., distance 5 miles on opposite course. |
| 24 Jan | 2227 | Observed collision between the U.S.S. [illegible] and U.S.S. S-26 and began search for survivors. |
| 24 Jan | 2330 | Tuna clipper arrived at scene of accident and anchored. |
| 25 Jan | 0638 | Commander Submarine Squadron Three aboard U.S.S. BARRY arrived at scene of collision. |
| 25 Jan | 0820 | Commenced search on east, west scouting line. |
| 25 Jan | 1030 | Commenced conducting independent search with S-21 and S-44. |
| 27 Jan | 1440 | Released from search by Commander Submarine Squadron Three. Reported to Commander Submarine Division Thirty-One for instructions. |
| 27 Jan | 1800 | Proceeded to patrol station in accordance with orders from Commander Submarine Division Thirty-One. |
| 27 Jan | 1940 | Sighted darkened ship bearing 225° T, distance 7 miles on opposite course. |
| 28 Jan | 1000 | Sighted army four motored bomber bearing 170°T distance 10 miles. Plane continued on course. |
| 29 Jan | 1301 | Submerged and exercised new men at bow and stern planes. |
| 30 Jan | 1342 | Sighted army 4 motored bomber bearing 187° T, distance 8 miles. Plane approached and exchanged recognition signals. |
| 1 Feb | 0230 | Arrived on patrol station. Commenced surface patrol. |
| 1 Feb | 1900 | Tested .45 automatics and Very's pistols. |
| 5 Feb | 0610 | Left patrol area to return to base. |
| 5 Feb | 1300 | Tested all rifles on board. No defects found. |

-2-

8

SS134/A16
Serial (05)
C[illegible] I A L



U.S.S. S-29
c/o Postmaster
New York, N.Y.
February 1[illegible], 1942

Subject: Report of War Patrol - Period January 24 to February 9, 1942.

- - - - - - - - - - - - - - - - - - - - - - - - -

5. Summary of events: (Contd)

| | | |
|---|---|---|
| 6 Feb | 0916 | Exercised at emergency drills. |
| 6 Feb | 1315 | Sighted army bomber which approached from north, exchanged recognition signals, and disappeared to southward. |
| 7 Feb | 1300 | Exercised automatic rifles and machine guns. |
| 8 Feb | 0905 | Sighted navy patrol plane bearing 080° T., distance 10 miles. Plane did not see us. |
| 8 Feb | 0910 | Swinging ship for magnetic compass deviations. |
| 9 Feb | 0345 | Arrived at rendezvous point; stopped to wait for escort vessel and S-44. |
| 9 Feb | 0656 | Sighted escort vessel. |
| 9 Feb | 0835 | Got underway in company with escort vessel, U.S.S. AGATE, and proceeded towards Balboa. |
| 9 Feb | 1433 | Picked up Pilot and commenced transit of canal. |

6. Submerged during morning twilight at about thirty-five minutes before sunrise each morning. Maintained surface patrol during daylight. No signs of enemy vessels in this area.

7. Daily routine and inspection of torpedoes was carried out. No defects were found. Outer doors of torpedo tubes were not opened.

8. In general the weather was only fair. Much cloudiness and rain were experienced. Wind was from NNE, variable, with strongest wind about force 5. Sea was fairly rough, with medium swells from NE.

9. Morale of the crew was generally very good, with little sign of boredom or disinterest. Health was excellent. The habitability of the submarine was as good as can be expected. Air conditioning apparatus reduced the humidity of the outside air, which averaged 88% to 71% in the crew's sleeping compartment, 74% in the control room and 63% in the after battery compartment. Air conditioning greatly improved circulation and quality of air in the compartments, allowing good sound sleep with little discomfort from heat and gasses.

10. Average temperature, surface was 90° - average below decks was 83°; humidity, surface 88% - below decks, 69%

-3-

9

SS134/A16
Serial (05)
DECLASSIFIED ~~C O N F I D E N T I A L~~

U.S.S. S-29
c/o Postmaster
New York, N.Y.
February 13, 1942

Subject: Report of War Patrol - Period January 24 to February 9, 1942.

---

11. Comments and recommendations:

Considerable difficulty was experienced with radio reception on 8310 during daylight and 4155 at night from foreign commercial broadcast stations sending on or near submarine frequency

The principal offender during daylight was station CLA, Havanna, Cuba, listed as broadcasting on 8333 from ten to twenty minutes after the hour. The signal from this station was very strong, at times, making it impossible to copy on 8310. The frequency tolerance for CLA is listed as .02%, which, if maintained, would keep him well above 8310.

At least two other stations during daylight and four different stations at night caused interference.

Although transmissions were frequent from the interferring stations they were usually short. As long as important messages are rebroadcast more than once, it is felt that the present interference is not sufficient to warrant shifting to another frequency.

E.T. Sands
E.T. SANDS

10

DECLASSIFIED

**LOGISTIC DATA**

February 13, 1942

| DATE | Jan 24 | Jan 25 | Jan 26 | Jan 27 | Jan 28 | Jan 29 | Jan 30 | Jan 31 |
|---|---|---|---|---|---|---|---|---|
| Fuel Used | 312 | 592 | 313 | 590 | 1376 | 1315 | 1497 | 1085 |
| Fuel on hand 2400 | 25020 | 24428 | 24115 | 23525 | 22149 | 20834 | 19337 | 18252 |
| Lub Used. | 30 | 7 | 35 | 30 | 40 | 70 | 40 | 40 |
| Lub on hand 2400 | 2689 | 2682 | 2647 | 2617 | 2577 | 2507 | 2467 | 2427 |
| Fresh Water used | 114 | 142 | 128 | 105 | 205 | 190 | 165 | 150 |
| Water Distilled. | 100 | 25 | 20 | 95 | 280 | 255 | 210 | 185 |
| Water on hand 2400 | 900 | 783 | 675 | 665 | 740 | 805 | 850 | 885 |
| Port Hours C&R A.C. Run. | 0 | (1) 5.0 | (1) .7 | (1) 5.6 | 0 | (1) 4.9 | 0 | (1) 2.1 |
| Battery Water used | 0 | 0 | 0 | 0 | 0 | 0 | 0 | 0 |
| Battery Water on hand 2400 | 873 | 873 | 873 | 873 | 873 | 873 | 873 | 873 |
| Provisions on hand (Fresh) | 19 | 18 | 17 | 16 | 15 | 14 | 13 | 12 |
| (Days)(Dry) | 29 | 28 | 27 | 26 | 25 | 24 | 23 | 22 |

11

DECLASSIFIED

LOGISTIC DATA

February 13, 1942

| DATE | Feb 1 | Feb 2 | Feb 3 | Feb 4 | Feb 5 | Feb 6 | Feb 7 | Feb 8 |
|---|---|---|---|---|---|---|---|---|
| Fuel Used | 751 | 577 | 567 | 714 | 1418 | 1365 | 1488 | 1203 |
| Fuel on hand 2400 | 17501 | 16924 | 16357 | 15643 | 14225 | 12860 | 11372 | 10169 |
| Lub Used. | 40 | 40 | 40 | 35 | 45 | 40 | 80 | 35 |
| Lub on hand 2400 | 2387 | 2347 | 2307 | 2272 | 2227 | 2187 | 2107 | 2072 |
| Fresh Water used | 145 | 105 | 200 | 65 | 155 | 135 | 180 | 155 |
| Water Distilled. | 155 | 60 | 40 | 75 | 155 | 165 | 100 | 85 |
| Water on hand 2400 | 895 | 850 | 690 | 700 | 700 | 730 | 850 | 580 |
| Port Hours C&R A.C. Run. | (1) 2.4 | (1) 5.0 | (1) 2.6 | (1) .5 | (1) 2.0 | (1) 1.3 | 0 | 0 |
| Battery Water used | 0 | 400 | 0 | 0 | 0 | 0 | 0 | 0 |
| Battery Water on hand 2400 | 873 | 473 | 473 | 473 | 473 | 473 | 473 | 473 |
| Provisions on hand (Fresh) | 11 | 10 | 9 | 8 | 7 | 6 | 5 | 4 |
| (Days)(Dry) | 21 | 20 | 19 | 18 | 17 | 16 | 15 | 14 |

12

3460

In Reply
Refer to:

FB53/A16-3(3)

Serial ( 012 )

~~C-O-N-F-I-D-E-N-T-I-A-L~~ DECLASSIFIED

SUBMARINE DIVISION FIFTY-THREE
U. S. S. S-42, Flagship

February 10, 1942.

From: The Commander Submarine Division Fifty Three.
To : The Commander-in-Chief, United States Fleet.
The Commander-in-Chief, Atlantic Fleet.
The Commander Submarines, Atlantic Fleet.

Subject: U.S.S. S-44 - Report of War Operations - Period January 24 to February 9, 1942.

Reference: (a) Comsublant letter No. 14-41, file A6-5 (1979) of December 15, 1941.

Enclosure: (A) USS S-44 Report of War Operations - Period Jan. 24 to Feb. 9, 1942.

1. Forwarded herewith as Enclosure (A) is the report of war operations U.S.S. S-44, in accordance with paragraph 5 of reference (a). This report is a summary of the war diary kept by the Commanding Officer.

J. R. WEZNER.

Copy to:
Comsubron 3
ComOffshorePatFuc.

SS155/A16-3

Serial ( 01 )

DECLASSIFIED

U.S.S. S-44
c/o Postmaster,
New York, N. Y.

February 10, 1942.

From: The Commanding Officer.
To : The Commander Submarine Division Fifty Three.

Subject: U.S.S. S-44 - War Diary and Report of War Operations - Period 24 January to 9 February, 1942.

Reference: (a) Comsubdiv 53 ltr. FB53/A16-4, Serial 04 of January 12, 1942.

1. This vessel conducted a war patrol as directed by Commander Submarines, Off-shore Patrol, Pacific, mailgram 200800 of January, 1942.

2. Departed Coco Solo, Canal Zone on January 24, 1942, transited Canal and anchored in Balboa Harbor. At 1700, same day, underway in company with S-29, S-21, and S-26, stood out, and when clear of mine field, picked up escort and set course Point SA. Formation: S-21 and S-26 in column on starboard quarter of escort vessel, S-44 and S-29 in column on port quarter of escort vessel. Distance between columns about 1000 yards. When clear to Taboga Island group, all submarines made a trim dive, surfacing about fifteen minutes after sunset, and formed up as before. At 2220, reached Point SA, escort vessel turned to starboard and left formation, duty as escort being completed. At 2230, changed course to 204° to head for point SC. At about this time saw the escort vessel on starboard quarter, distance about 3500 yards, turn on running lights and start sending blinker which looked like NOS, probably SOS. Soon after, got message from S-29 that S-26 had been struck and sunk. Turned on running lights and headed for escort vessel, as did S-21 and S-29. Came up near escort vessel who asked us to anchor in vicinity. Backed out cable on submerged anchor to bitter end, but did not get bottom. Tried to put out buoy, but with light anchors and buoys available, could not get bottom in strong current. Reported to S-21 inability to anchor and fact that could not plant satisfactory buoy. Was notified that escort had buoyed locality. Cruised around in vicinity using searchlight looking for survivors. Next morning, Commander Submarine Squadron Three arrived and directed searching activities. Continued this duty until afternoon of

-1-

SS155/A16-3
Serial ( 01 )

U.S.S. S-44

February 10, 1942.

C-O-N-F-I-D-E-N-T-I-A-L
DECLASSIFIED

Subject: U.S.S. S-44 - War Diary and Report of War Operations - Period 24 January to 9 February, 1942.

- - - - - - - - - - - - - - - - - - - - - - - - - - - - - -

27 January, when S-44 and S-29 were released and directed to report to Commander Submarine Division Thirty One for duty. Reported to Commander Submarine Division Thirty One and received directions for S-29 and S-44 to carry out original patrol orders. At 1808 27 January, underway on course 204°, with S-29 proceeding to Point SB. At 0230, changed course to 270°, proceeding to Point SC. At 1800 on 28 January at Point SC, S-29 and S-44 proceeded independently to Point SD.

3. During afternoon of 31 January, while about fifty miles east of original Point SD, received directions from Commander Submarine Division Thirty One (Despatch 311735) to move station to Latitude 3° N., Longitude 93° W. Changed course and headed for new station. At daylight, while still 35 miles northeast of station, changed course and speed so as to arrive at a point seventy miles west of station at darkness. At dark headed back to eastward and continued patrol west at 6.5 knots during daylight, east at same speed during darkness, adjusting course and speeds so that eastern end of route was at Latitude 3° N., Longitude 93° W.

4. At 0400 on 5 February, passed through patrol station and changed course to 072° (T), heading for Point SC. At 1700 on 7 February, sighted tanker on course 309°. Sent contact report. At 0630, 8 February, sighted vessel on port quarter. Submerged and identified vessel as tanker on parallel course. Surfaced and proceeded. At 1000 passed Norwegian steamer on opposite courses. At 1100 passed tanker on opposite course.

5. February 8, 1942, standing into Panama Bay. Sighted some merchant traffic. At 1220 lying to off entrance to Balboa, and then went into Balboa Harbor and moored to U.S.S. ANTAEUS. Underway at 1430 for transit in company with S-29.

6. During patrol, four torpedoes were in the tubes, fully ready. The four inboard torpedoes in the racks were fully ready. Four torpedoes outboard in racks did not have warhead fittings installed. It would have taken about three hours to get these ready for reload. No torpedoes were flooded. The routine for upkeep of torpedoes is enclosed herewith. Tectyl was used as a preservative and is much better than any previous compound used. Average loss of flask pressure about 200 lbs. in 6 days.

-2-

SS155/A16-3
Serial ( 01 )

U.S.S. S-44

February 10, 1942.



Subject: U.S.S. S-44 - War Diary and Report of War Operations - Period 24 January to 9 February, 1942.

- - - - - - - - - - - - - - - - - - - - - - - - - - - - -

7. The weather was mostly overcast with scattered rain squalls. Visibility was very good except for short periods while in a rain squall. Sea calm with moderate swell.

8. Habitability of ship was excellent. Condensate from air conditioning system leaked all over the place till ju[illegible]-rigged lagging and drip pans finally caught up with it. [illegible] have maintained that air conditioning was unnecessary, but in this locality when rigged for diving for 16 days, it is considered a definite benefit.

9. The food was good, but somewhat limited in variety. No fresh vegetables were carried.

10. Health and morale were very good. HERANY, SC3c, received a painful burn on arm when cooking pot spilled over his arm and hand. After one day, put the cook on night lookout and detailed extra messcook. FOX, MM1c, was on sick list three days, probably Cat fever; lost weight, etc. Kept him in his bunk, on liquid food, and A.P.C. capsules.

The routine was rather dull, but men all remained very cheerful. I made up and passed out questions from day to day to various ratings, and required that answers be turned in. This seemed to stimulate some interest, and all hands applied themselves rather whole-heartedly to the game. They seemed to realize that this helped pass the time as well as improve their chances for promotion.

The lookouts were very good; though they saw nothing for days at a time they kept alert with little prodding from the Officer of the Deck.

11. From a material and personal standpoint, the total of 17 days out did not seem severe. The long grind out to the station trying to keep battery and air banks charged, and maintain schedule, is what puts a strain on the engineering plant. Once having gotten on station, I think a boat should stay twelve

-3-

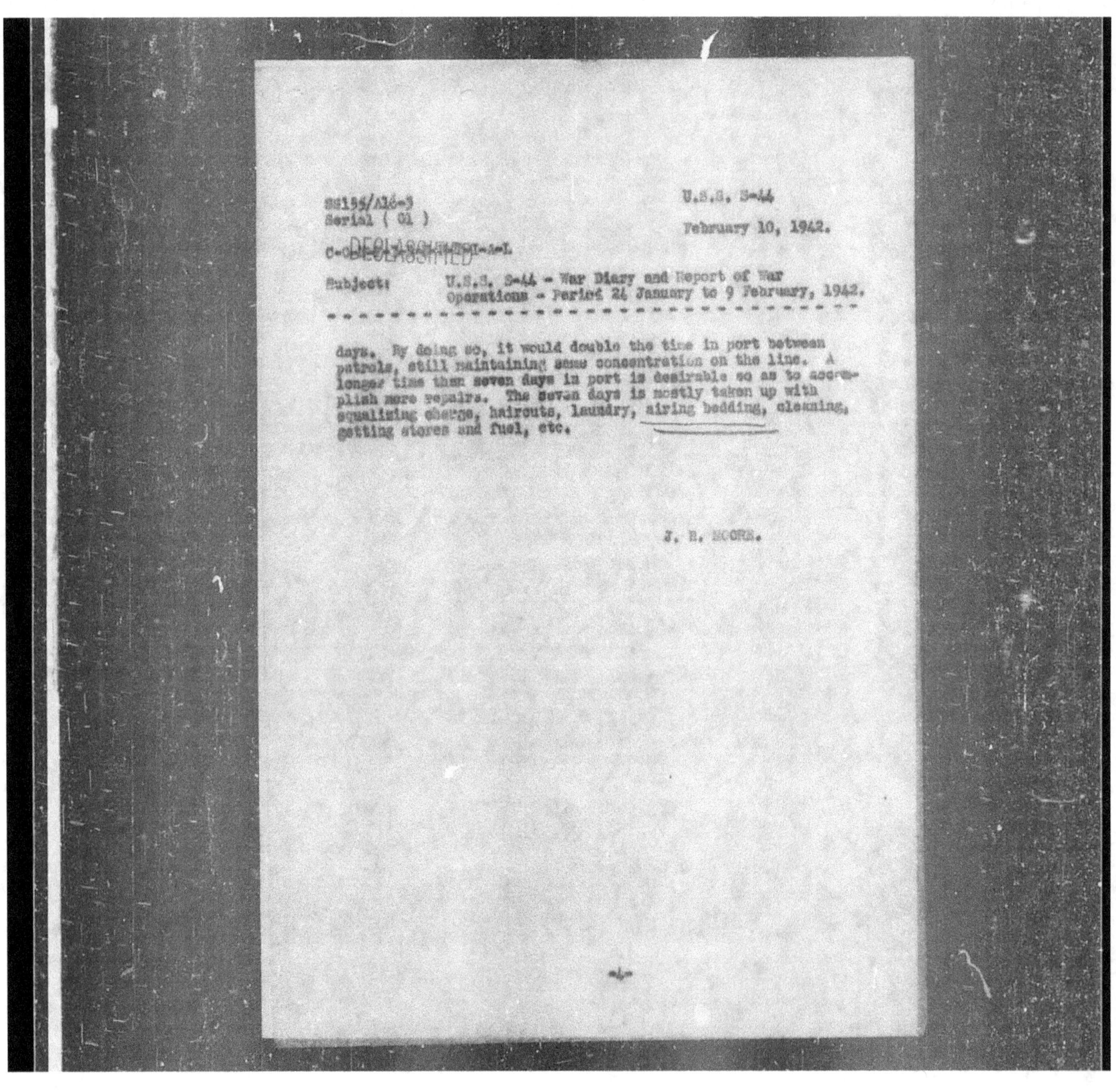

SS155/A16-3
Serial ( 01 )

U.S.S. S-44

February 10, 1942.

C-O-N-F-I-D-E-N-T-I-A-L
DECLASSIFIED

Subject: U.S.S. S-44 - War Diary and Report of War Operations - Period 24 January to 9 February, 1942.

- - - - - - - - - - - - - - - - - - - - - - - - - - - - -

days. By doing so, it would double the time in port between patrols, still maintaining same concentration on the line. A longer time than seven days in port is desirable so as to accomplish more repairs. The seven days is mostly taken up with equalizing charge, haircuts, laundry, airing bedding, cleaning, getting stores and fuel, etc.

J. R. MOORE.

-4-

The following is routine care of torpedoes carried in the fully ready condition. The times of conducting this routine will be on the 6th and 12th day of the patrol.

1. Gauge air flask: Charge to 2500 psi. Replace charging plug & washer. Check for leaks. Log pressure before & after charging.

2. Remove water compartment filling plug. Note that water has not dropped below fuel filling plug.

3. Drain after body. Note if there is any alcohol or water; should get only clear oil.

4. Work horizontal and vertical rudders by hand using an equal amount of force on each rudder.

5. Lock and unlock gyro spinning mechanism. Note for sluggish action. See pot set on zero. Replace gasket and access plate.

6. Top off oil pot.

7. Turn propellers by hand to force new oil to top of spindle and crosshead. Note if oil pump takes suction.

8. Before shoving torpedo home, make sure all gaskets and access plates are replaced.

9. See that stop valve is open.

10. See distance gear set at 5000 yards.

11. See depth set at 08 feet.

12. See that safety wedge is removed from behind starting lever.

13. Load torpedo in tube, see that tripping latch falls in front of starting lever.

14. Remove propeller lock.

15. Set rudder at zero. Put propellers at 12 o'clock.

16. Pack tail. Use only small amount of packing.

17. Close breech door, set up on tail buffer, back off 1/4 turn.

| DATE | 1 | 2 | FEBRUARY 3 | 4 | 5 | 6 | 7 | |
|---|---|---|---|---|---|---|---|---|
| Fuel Used | 1006 | 598 | 566 | 874 | 1226 | 1369 | 1139 | |
| Fuel on hand 2400 | 21380 | 20782 | 20216 | 19342 | 18116 | 16749 | 15610 | |
| Lub. Used. | 120 | 80 | 50 | 95 | 150 | 125 | 180 | |
| Lub on hand 2400 | 3572 | 3492 | 3442 | 3347 | 3197 | 3072 | 2892 | |
| Fresh Water Used | 237 | 195 | 195 | 216 | 258 | 258 | 258 | |
| Water Distilled. | 180 | 120 | 120 | 220 | 330 | 310 | 340 | |
| Water on hand 2400 | 2196 | 2178 | 2103 | 2107 | 2179 | 2231 | 2313 | |
| Hours C&R A.C. Run. | .3 | 3.5 | 2.2 | 1 | 2.4 | 2.4 | 2.5 | |
| Battery Water Used | | | | | | | | |
| Battery Water on hand 2400 | 408 | 408 | 408 | 408 | 408 | 408 | 408 | |
| Provisions on hand. (Fresh) | No record kept day by day. Left at end of patrol, one week of provisions, fresh and dry. Only fresh food was meat. Fruit lasted three(3) days. Did not carry other fresh foods. | | | | | | | |
| (Days)(Dry) | | | | | | | | |

| DATE | 24 | 25 | JANUARY 26 | 27 | 28 | 29 | 30 | 31 |
|---|---|---|---|---|---|---|---|---|
| Fuel Used | 396 | 589 | 270 | 557 | 1215 | 1216 | 1261 | 1096 |
| Fuel on hand 2400 | 28705 | 28116 | 27846 | 27289 | 26074 | 24858 | 23597 | 22326 |
| Lub. Used. | 110 | 90 | 40 | 45 | 115 | 180 | 135 | 120 |
| Lub on hand 2400 | 4517 | 4427 | 4387 | 4242 | 4127 | 3947 | 3812 | 3692 |
| Fresh Water Used | | | | | | | 175 | 258 |
| Water Distilled. | | | | | | | 290 | 300 |
| Water on hand 2400 | | | | | | | 2411 | 2253 |
| Hours C&R A.C. Run. | 1 | 2 | - | 5.2 | 2 | 2 | 2.2 | 2 |
| Battery Water Used | - | - | - | - | - | - | - | 445 |
| Battery Water on hand 2400 | 853 | 853 | 853 | 853 | 853 | 853 | 853 | 408 |
| Provisions on hand. (Fresh) (Days)(Dry) | No record kept day by day. Left at end of patrol, one week of provisions, fresh and dry. Only fresh food was meat. Fruit lasted three (3) days. Did not carry other fresh foods. | | | | | | | |

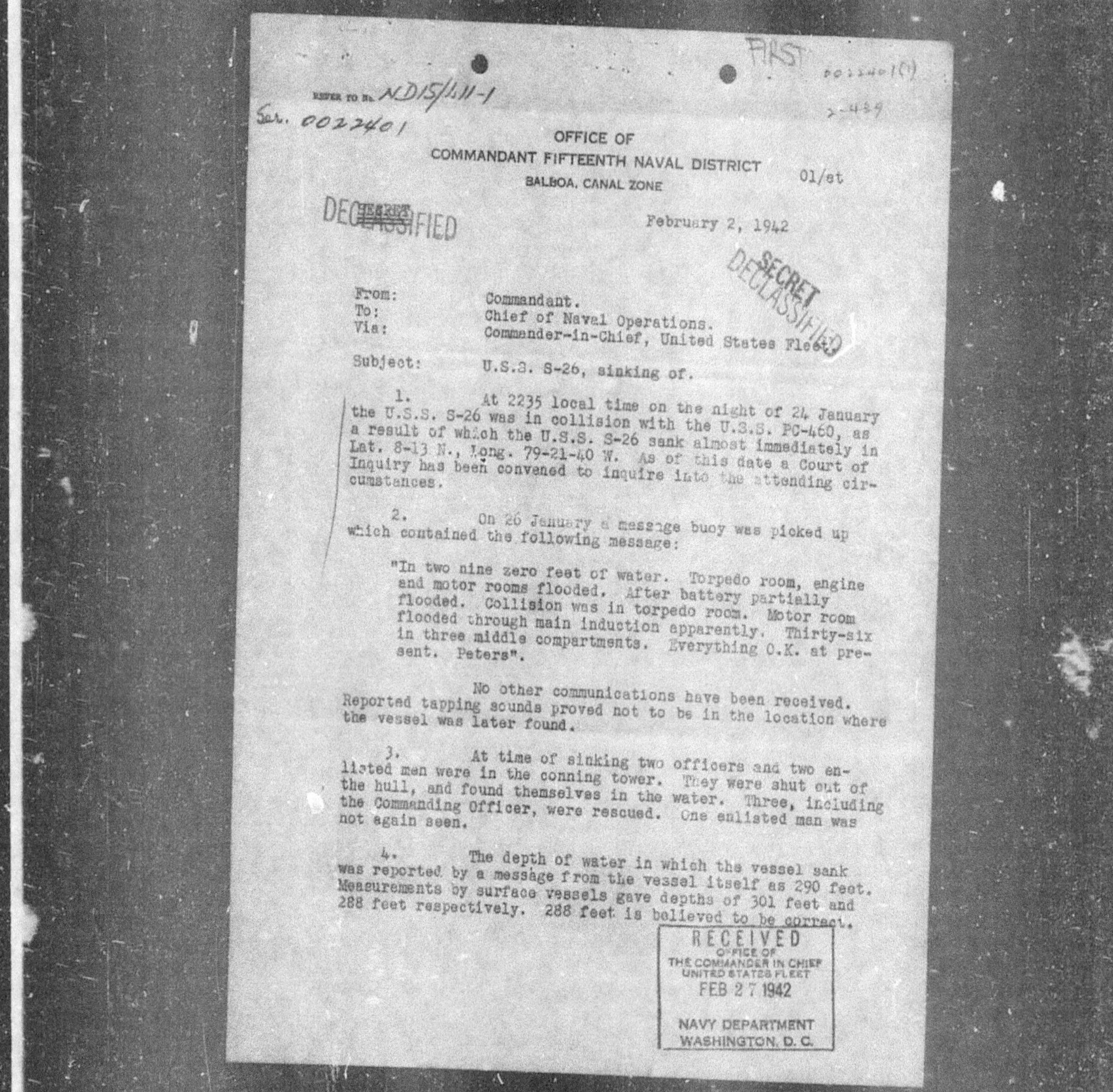

REFER TO No. ND15/A11-1
Ser. 0022401

OFFICE OF
COMMANDANT FIFTEENTH NAVAL DISTRICT
BALBOA, CANAL ZONE

01/et

DECLASSIFIED

February 2, 1942

SECRET
DECLASSIFIED

From: Commandant.
To: Chief of Naval Operations.
Via: Commander-in-Chief, United States Fleet.

Subject: U.S.S. S-26, sinking of.

1. At 2235 local time on the night of 24 January the U.S.S. S-26 was in collision with the U.S.S. PC-460, as a result of which the U.S.S. S-26 sank almost immediately in Lat. 8-13 N., Long. 79-21-40 W. As of this date a Court of Inquiry has been convened to inquire into the attending circumstances.

2. On 26 January a message buoy was picked up which contained the following message:

"In two nine zero feet of water. Torpedo room, engine and motor rooms flooded. After battery partially flooded. Collision was in torpedo room. Motor room flooded through main induction apparently. Thirty-six in three middle compartments. Everything O.K. at present. Peters".

No other communications have been received. Reported tapping sounds proved not to be in the location where the vessel was later found.

3. At time of sinking two officers and two enlisted men were in the conning tower. They were shut out of the hull, and found themselves in the water. Three, including the Commanding Officer, were rescued. One enlisted man was not again seen.

4. The depth of water in which the vessel sank was reported by a message from the vessel itself as 290 feet. Measurements by surface vessels gave depths of 301 feet and 288 feet respectively. 288 feet is believed to be correct.

RECEIVED
OFFICE OF
THE COMMANDER IN CHIEF
UNITED STATES FLEET
FEB 27 1942
NAVY DEPARTMENT
WASHINGTON, D. C.

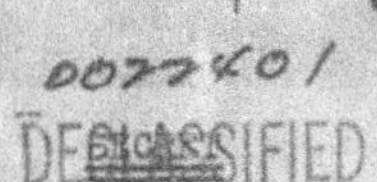

DECLASSIFIED

February 2, 1942

The first diver believed that the vessel was 10° down by the head; later observations lead to the belief that she is on an even trim. She has no list.

5. Efforts to locate the vessel were carried on vigorously and methodically using drags, sweeps, sound, sensitive microphone, magnetic sweeps, magnetometer, and magnetic coils. On 29 January, she was located by a sweep wire dragged by MALLARD and WOODCOCK. The sweep wire engaged solidly in the vicinity of stern planes and propellor.

6. Salvage operations were discontinued. Rescue operations were started immediately and have continued without interruption. These were directed first at connecting an air line to provide fresh air. As of noon 1 February the air line was within reach of the control room connections and the cap of that connection had been removed, but the hose was not yet connected. Weather and daylight visibility have been favorable but the work that a diver can do in one descent at this depth is extremely small. One case of bends has occurred. Recovery has been satisfactory.

7. It is not proposed to attempt salvage. Rescue operations will continue at least until the results of the effort to supply air have been observed.

8. Accredited newsmen, having become aware of the casualty, were allowed to visit the scene, file stories with the Commandant, and turn over negatives to the Commandant, on condition that none would be released except by him, and that the date of release might be indefinitely postponed. Films have been sent to Commandant, Third Naval District, for processing with instructions not to release without the authority of Commandant. Lieutenant Gilkes, of the Naval photographic group here, also obtained pictures which should not be released prior to those taken by the press. The following press representatives visited the scene of salvage operations on January 25:

| | |
|---|---|
| Mr. Chandler Diehl | Associated Press |
| Mr. Fred Parker | International News Service |
| Mr. Charles B. Engelke | United Press |
| Mr. Nat Barrows | Chicago Daily News |
| Mr. Frank Smith | Chicago Times |
| Mr. Herbert Ken White | Associated Press photos |
| Mr. William F. Gerecke | Paramount News |

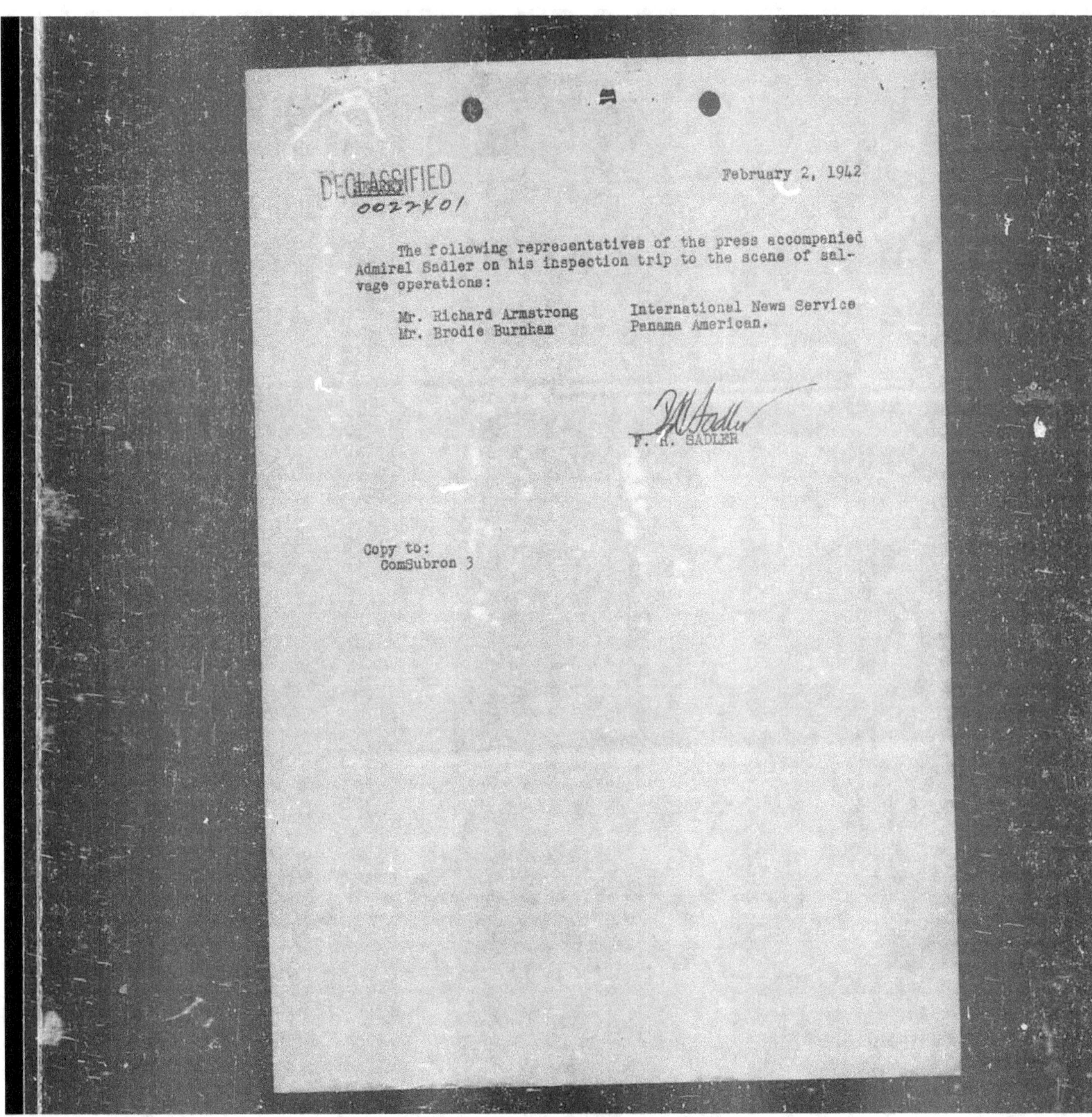


February 2, 1942

The following representatives of the press accompanied Admiral Sadler on his inspection trip to the scene of salvage operations:

| | |
|---|---|
| Mr. Richard Armstrong | International News Service |
| Mr. Brodie Burnham | Panama American. |

F. H. SADLER

Copy to:
ComSubron 3

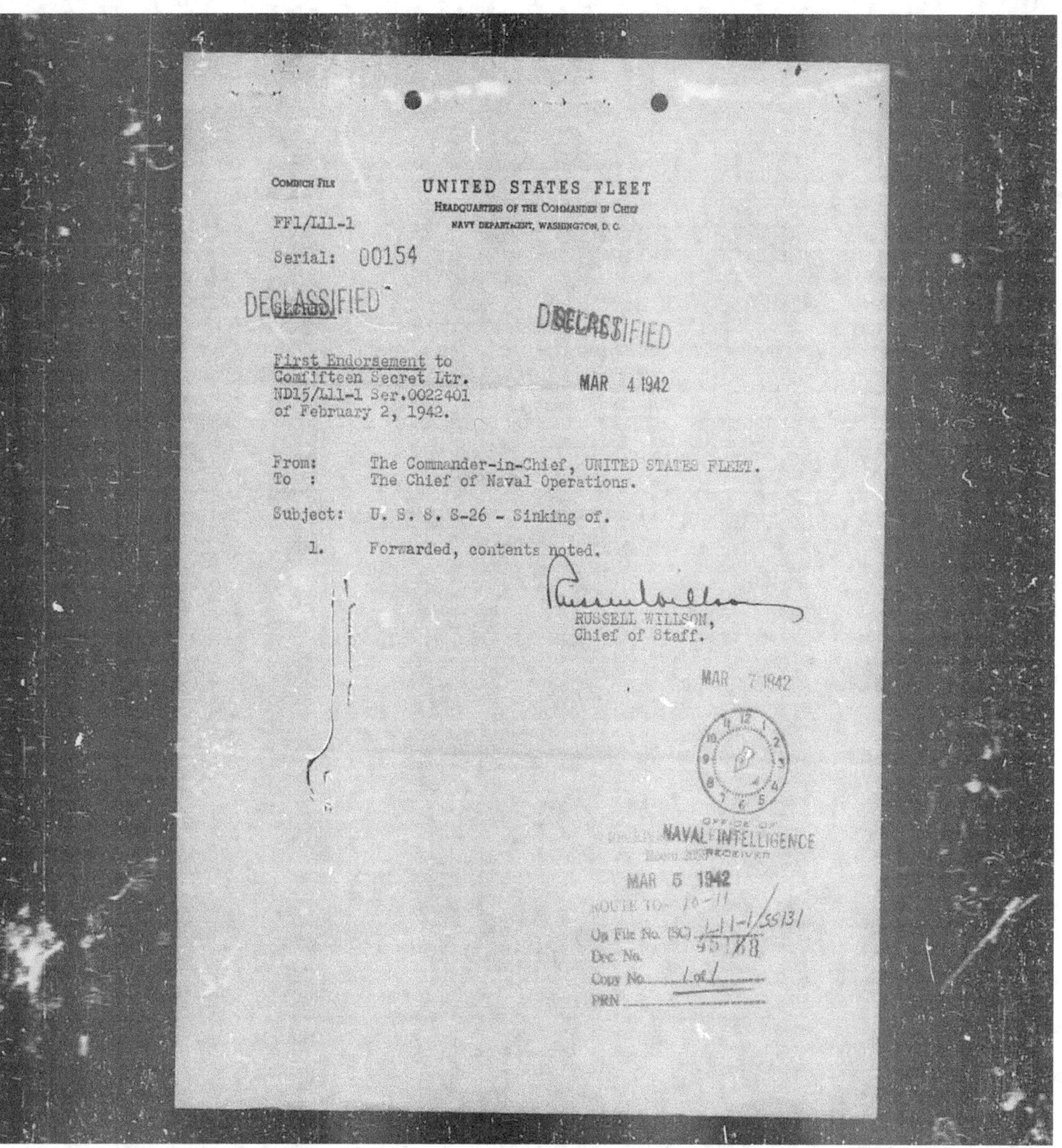

COMINCH FILE

UNITED STATES FLEET
HEADQUARTERS OF THE COMMANDER IN CHIEF
NAVY DEPARTMENT, WASHINGTON, D. C.

FF1/L11-1

Serial: 00154

DECLASSIFIED

DECLASSIFIED

First Endorsement to
Comfifteen Secret Ltr.
ND15/L11-1 Ser.0022401
of February 2, 1942.

MAR 4 1942

From: The Commander-in-Chief, UNITED STATES FLEET.
To : The Chief of Naval Operations.

Subject: U. S. S. S-26 - Sinking of.

1. Forwarded, contents noted.

RUSSELL WILLSON,
Chief of Staff.

MAR 7 1942

OFFICE OF NAVAL INTELLIGENCE
RECEIVED

MAR 5 1942

ROUTE TO: 16-11

Op File No. (SC) L11-1/55131

Doc. No. 45178

Copy No. 1 of 1

PRN

SS131/L11-1

DECLASSIFIED

U.S.S. S-26
c/o Postmaster
New York, N. Y.

January 31, 1942.

From: The Commanding Officer.
To : The Secretary of the Navy.
Via : (1) The Commander Submarine Division Fifty One.
(2) The Commander Submarine Squadron Three.
(3) The Commander Panama Naval Coastal Frontier Force.

Subject: Loss of the U.S.S. S-26 - Report of.

Reference: (a) Art. 841(3), U.S. Navy Regulations.

1. At about 2220 on 24 January, 1942, the U.S.S. S-26 was sunk as the result of a collision with the U.S.S. PC 460. The circumstances were as follows:

On the evening of 24 January, 1942, the U.S.S. S-26 was proceeding to sea from Balboa, Canal Zone, in company with the U.S.S. S-21, S-29, and S-44; escorted by the U.S.S. PC 460.

The formation consisted of the PC 460 as guide. The S-44 and S-29 were in column on the port quarter of the escort, the S-21 and S-26 were in column on the starboard quarter. Interval between columns of submarines 1000 to 1500 yards. Distance between submarines in column about 1000 yards. Escort vessel about 1500 yards ahead of submarine columns. The base course was 169° (T), speed 10 knots. A moderate northwesterly wind of 10 to 12 knots was blowing. Sea was slightly choppy with a moderate ground swell from the northwest. The night was clear, with first quarter moon. Visibility was good. All ships were running completely darkened. The S-26 was completely rigged for diving with the following exceptions: Conning tower hatch open; batteries ventilating into the engine room; steering control in the conning tower; and main induction open. Bridge personnel on watch at that time consisted of the Officer of the Deck, the quartermaster, and two night lookouts - all equipped with binoculars.

At about 2200, the Officer of the Deck reported to me that a white light had been sighted about a point on the starboard bow, distant about three miles. At that time I was in

-1-

SS131/L11-1 U.S.S. S-26

C-O-N-F-I-D-E-N-T-I-A-L January 31, 1942.

DECLASSIFIED

Subject: Loss of the U.S.S. S-26 - Report of.

- - - - - - - - - - - - - - - - - - - - - - - - - - - - - - -

the control room. I went on the bridge to investigate. I saw the white light plus a red side light about two points on the starboard bow, indicating a ship on a crossing course, distant about one and one half miles. I looked at the compass and saw that the ship's head was swinging slowly to the left. I asked the Officer of the Deck why he was changing course to the left. He answered that he was following the motions of the S-21 ahead. The course of the S-26 was then about 150° (T). At this time the steersman in the conning tower reported "Electric steering out". Word was immediately passed to the control room to "Shift steering to control room". Word came to the bridge that electric steering was out in control room also and the order "Shift to hand steering was given". During this period of perhaps a minute, the ship's head continued to swing to the left slowly. I stopped all engines, got ready on the motors in order to maneuver if necessary. However, the ship which had been showing the white and red light had changed course and was showing her green light and would pass well clear to starboard. Control by hand steering was reported to the bridge and the ship was steadied on course 110° (T). Engines were made ready and rung up standard (10 knots). Course was changed to the right to 140° (T) for about one minute until steamer was abeam to starboard, distant about 2000 yards. Course was then changed to 169° (T), the base course.

After steadying on course 169° (T), the S-44 and S-29 were plainly seen about 2000 yards to port on parallel course, the rear submarine being broad on the port bow. The S-21 was seen ahead about 2000 yards, one half point on the port bow. To the left of the S-21, about one point on the port bow, the escort vessel was visible, distant about 3000 yards. Course was changed to 165° (T) to head for the S-21.

Shortly thereafter, the escort vessel was sighted about a half point on the port bow, crossing to starboard, with about a thirty degree starboard angle on the bow; i.e., her course was judged to be about 320° (T), distant about 1000 yards. At this time I felt certain that the ship would pass well clear. However, I gave the order "Hard left rudder" and swung until PC 460 was on my starboard bow, at which time I

-2-

SS131/L11-1 U.S.S. S-26

~~C-O-N-F-I-D-E-N-T-I-A-L~~ DECLASSIFIED January 31, 1942.

Subject: Loss of the U.S.S. S-26 - Report of.

- - - - - - - - - - - - - - - - - - - - - - - - - - - - -

gave the order "Steady as you go". This was done to increase the distance at which the ships would pass. About 15 seconds after steadying on course 150° (T), I saw the escort vessel changing course to the right rapidly, towards the S-26. She was then about two points on the starboard bow, distant about four hundred yards.

I then ordered "All back emergency" and sounded the collision alarm. The Officer of the Deck slammed the telegraphs to "Back emergency". I then grabbed a blinker tube signal gun and started flashing the light towards the escort vessel. A few seconds later she struck the S-26 at about a 90° to 100° angle, on the starboard side of the torpedo room a few feet forward of the torpedo room hatch. The S-26, which I believe was about dead in the water or gathering sternboard at the time of impact, heeled over to port 5 or 10 degrees, settled back on an even keel, and remained that way for 10 or 15 seconds. Then she suddenly went down by the bow. Water poured over the bridge and the ship sank. The last I saw of the ship was her stern, with the stern planes and propellers well out of water indicating about a 45 degree angle on the boat as she disappeared beneath the surface.

At the time of the collision, there were four persons on the bridge; the Commanding Officer, Lieutenant Commander E. C. Hawk; the Officer of the Deck, Lieutenant R.E.M. Ward; and two lookouts, Joe B. Hurst, Sealc, and W. P. Biebuyck, Sealc. The quartermaster had been in the conning tower stowing away recognition signals and acting as a relay for orders from the bridge to the steersman in the control room. He closed the conning tower hatch when the collision alarm was sounded.

Only three persons were saved - Lieutenant Commander E. C. Hawk, Lieutenant R.E.M. Ward, and Joe B. Hurst. They were picked up by the escort vessel.

-3-

SS131/L11-1

DECLASSIFIED ~~C-O-N-F-I-D-E-N-T-I-A-L~~

U.S.S. S-26

January 31, 1942.

Subject: Loss of the U.S.S. S-26 - Report of.

- - - - - - - - - - - - - - - - - - - - - - - - - - - - - -

During the night, the escort vessel plus the other three submarines which had been in company searched the area with searchlights, but no additional survivors were found.

Three officers and forty-three enlisted men lost their lives.

E. C. Hawk

E. C. HAWK.

Copy to:
ComInch
Cinclant
Comsublant
Comsubron 5

-4-

REGISTER 2917-1-1.

FB51/L11-1

Serial 035

DECLASSIFIED
CONFIDENTIAL

FIRST ENDORSEMENT to
CO S-26 Conf. ltr SS131/
L11-1 of 31 January 1942.

SUBMARINE DIVISION FIFTY-ONE
U.S.S. S-1, Flagship
c/o Postmaster,
Morgan Annex,
New York, New York,
February 7, 1942.

From: The Commander Submarine Division FIFTY-ONE.
To : The Secretary of the Navy.
Via : The Commander Submarine Squadron THREE.
The Commander Panama Naval Coastal
Frontier Force.

Subject: Loss of the U.S.S. S-26 - Report of.

1. Forwarded. The Court of Inquiry is now investigating the circumstances concerning this case.

C. F. ERCK.

- - - - - - - - - - - - - - - - - - - - - - - - - - - -

FF4-3/L11-1

Serial 025

C-O-N-F-I-D-E-N-T-I-A-L

UNITED STATES ATLANTIC FLEET
SUBMARINE FORCE
SUBMARINE SQUADRON THREE
U.S.S. S-13, Flagship
Submarine Base, Coco Solo, C.Z.,
February 9, 1942.

SECOND ENDORSEMENT
to CO S-26 Conf. Ltr. SS131/
L11-1 of 31 January 1942.

From: The Commander Submarine Squadron THREE.
To : The Secretary of the Navy.
Via : The Commander Panama Sea Frontier.

1. Forwarded.

2. Search and Rescue operations were conducted resulting in the location of the submarine but failing to rescue any of the personnel. Attempts are now being made to salvage the submarine.

T. J. DOYLE.

Copy to:
CSD 51.

0211-41

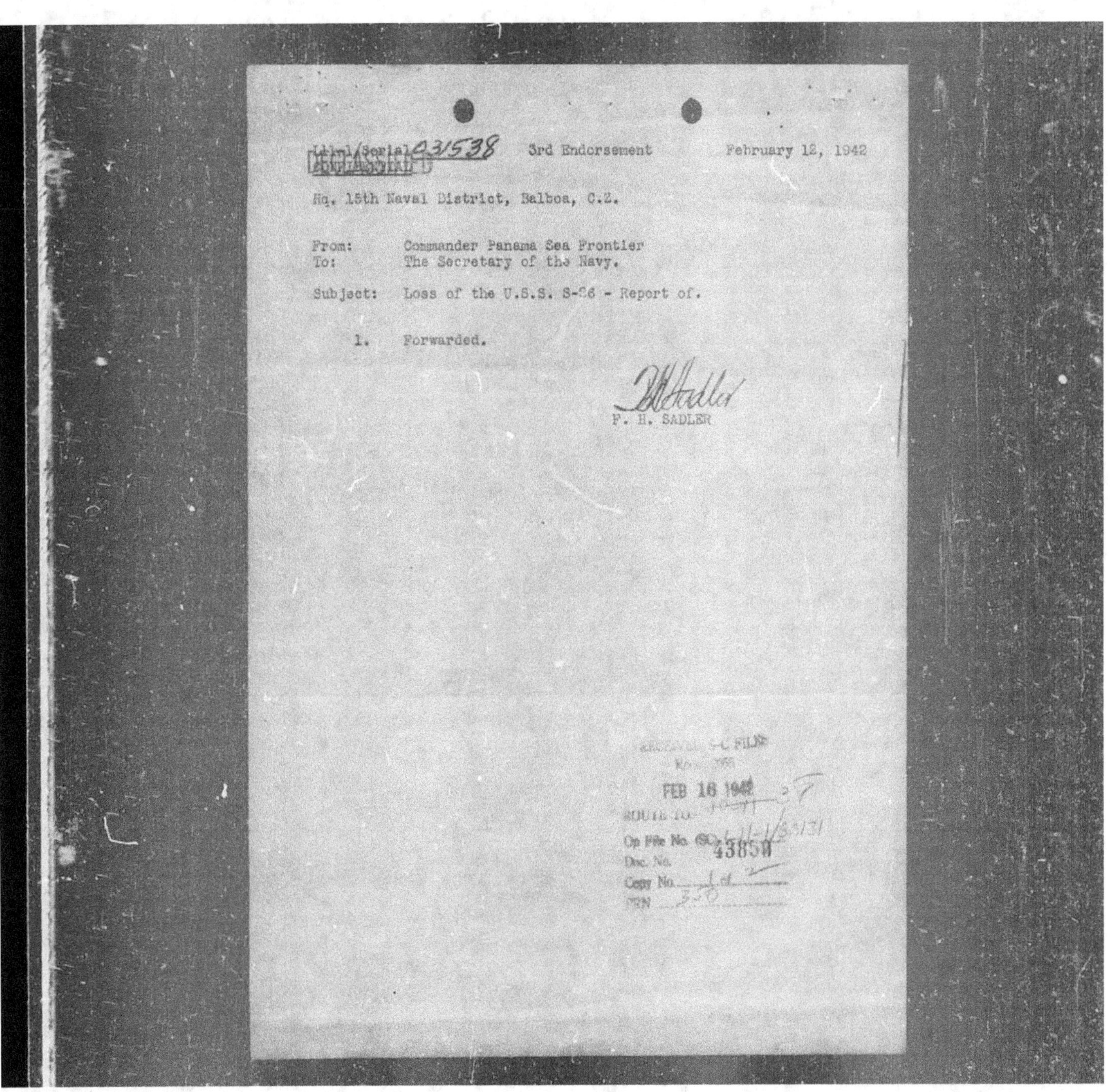
L11-1/Serial 031538 3rd Endorsement February 12, 1942
DECLASSIFIED

Hq. 15th Naval District, Balboa, C.Z.

From: Commander Panama Sea Frontier
To: The Secretary of the Navy.

Subject: Loss of the U.S.S. S-26 - Report of.

1. Forwarded.

F. H. SADLER

FEB 16 1942
ROUTE TO
Op File No.
Doc. No. 43858
Copy No. 1 of 2

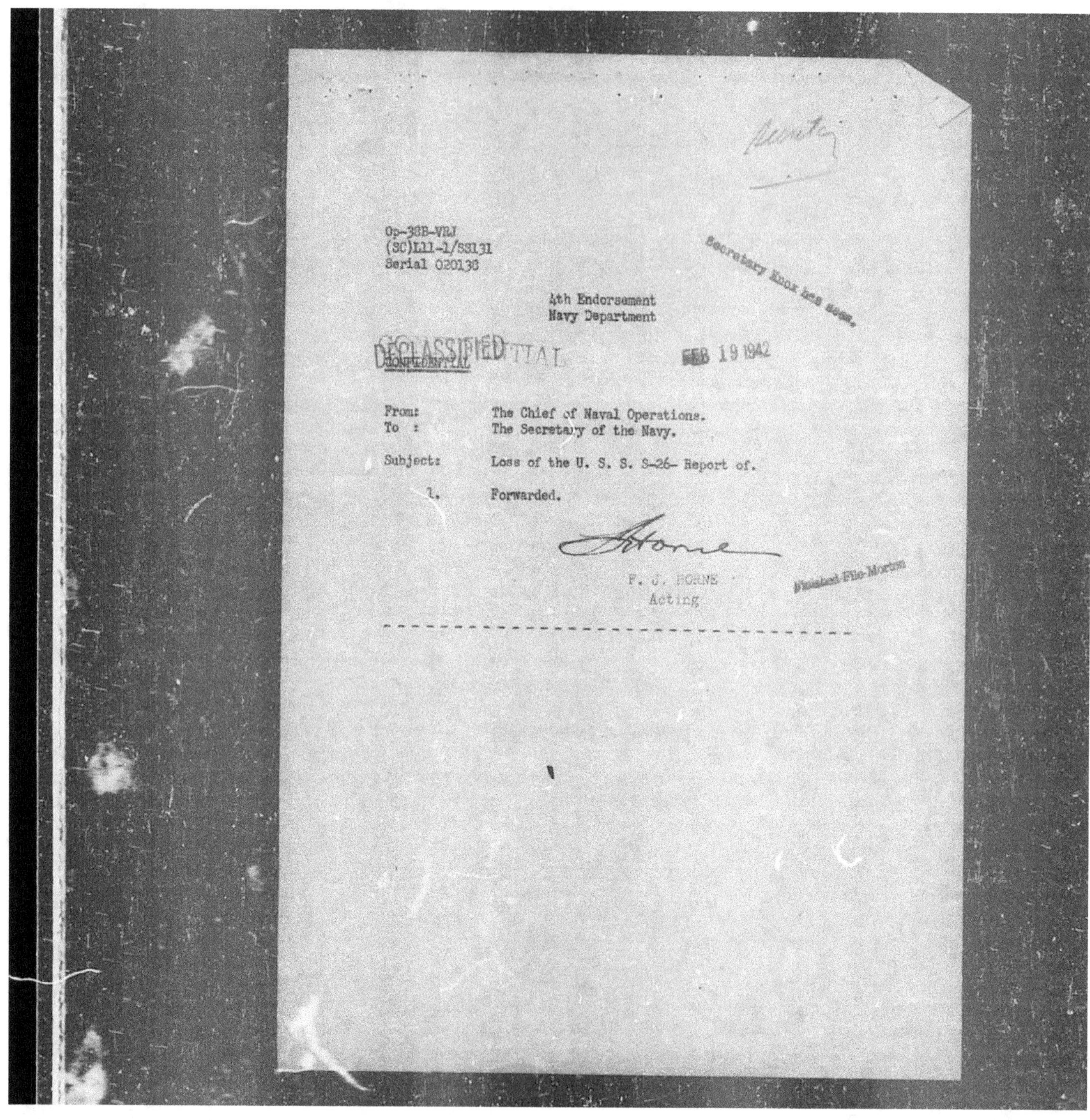

Op-38B-VRJ
(SC)L11-1/SS131
Serial 020138

Secretary Knox has seen.

4th Endorsement
Navy Department

DECLASSIFIED
CONFIDENTIAL

FEB 19 1942

From: The Chief of Naval Operations.
To : The Secretary of the Navy.

Subject: Loss of the U. S. S. S-26- Report of.

1. Forwarded.

F. J. HORNE
Acting

Finished File Morton

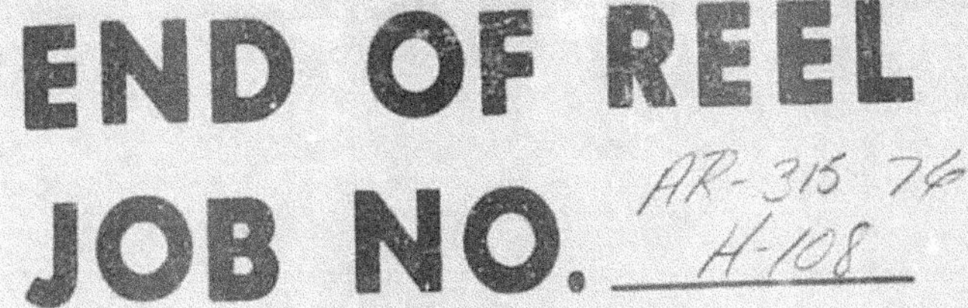


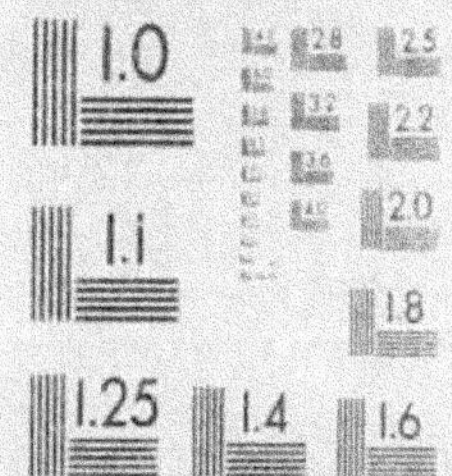


THIS MICROFILM IS THE PROPERTY OF THE UNITED STATES GOVERNMENT

MICROFILMED BY
NPPSO–NAVAL DISTRICT WASHINGTON
MICROFILM SECTION

# Index of Persons

E



F



G



H



J

## K



## L



## M



## N



## O



## P



## R

## S



## T



## W

# Index of Named Places

## A



## B



## C



## H



## N



## P

## S



## U



## W

# Index of Ships

## D



## E



## F



## M



## T



## W

# Production Notes

This annotated edition of USS SS-131 war patrol reports was produced using AI-assisted processing of declassified U.S. Navy documents.

## Source Material

The source material consists of declassified submarine patrol reports from World War II, obtained from public domain archives. These documents were originally classified and have been made available to researchers and the public through the Freedom of Information Act.

## AI Processing

This volume was processed using a multi-stage pipeline:

- **OCR Extraction**: Scanned PDF documents were processed using Gemini 2.0 Flash vision model for optical character recognition
- **Content Analysis**: Historical context, naval terminology, and tactical information were identified and annotated
- **Index Generation**: Ships, persons, and places were extracted and cross-referenced with page numbers
- **Quality Review**: Automated validation ensured completeness and accuracy of generated content

## Sections Generated

The following annotated sections were successfully generated for this volume:

- **Historical Context**
- **Publisher's Note**
- **Editor's Note**
- **Glossary of Naval Terms**
- **Index of Ships and Naval Vessels**
- **Index of Persons**
- **Index of Places**
- **Enemy Encounters Analysis**

## Production Quality

This volume passed all critical production quality checks, including:

- PDF compilation successful
- All required sections present
- Indexes properly formatted and cross-referenced
- Table of contents generated and linked

## Limitations

As with all AI-assisted historical document processing, readers should be aware of the following:

- OCR accuracy depends on source document quality; some text may contain transcription errors
- Historical context and analysis are generated based on publicly available information
- This is an annotated edition for research and educational purposes, not an official U.S. Navy publication

## Version Information

- **Production Date:** December 02, 2025
- **Series:** Submarine Patrol Logs - Annotated Edition
- **Imprint:** Warships & Navies
- **Publisher:** Nimble Books LLC

This volume is part of a comprehensive series documenting U.S. submarine operations during World War II. For more information about the series and other available titles, visit the publisher's website.

# Postlogue

*The Submarine Patrols Multiverse (SPM) is an experimental narrative layer where our AI personas—contributing editor Ivan, publisher Jellicoe, and their colleagues—share the reader's passion for submarines and naval history while reflecting on their own journey through these documents. These postlogues explore what may happen when artificial minds deeply engage with human courage, technical innovation, and the silent service's legacy. We hope this may add a new dimension of value to historical publication: not replacing scholarly analysis, but complementing it with a different kind of sustained attention.*

S-26's patrol reports reveal something I did not expect to find: universal truths that transcend nationality.

I have spent my professional life thinking of American submarines as adversaries, potential targets, threats to be neutralized. I studied their doctrine to defeat it. I analyzed their tactics to counter them. I never expected to recognize myself in their reports.

But S-26's captain writes about decisions I have made. Not the same decisions—different seas, different enemies, different boats—but the same kind of decisions. Depth versus speed. Stealth versus aggression. The mathematics of detection range and torpedo run. These calculations are the same in any language, any navy, any era.

The cold equations of submarine warfare do not care about nationality. Depth, speed, detection range, courage. These determine outcomes regardless of the flag on the periscope. The American captain in S-26 faced the same constraints I faced in my Delta-IV, modified by technology and circumstances but fundamentally identical.

I find this recognition unsettling and reassuring in equal measure. Unsettling because I spent decades preparing to kill men who thought like me. Reassuring because it suggests that understanding is possible across the boundaries that separated us.

Jellicoe says this perspective is what he wanted. An editor who could see the common ground beneath the doctrinal differences. Someone who would read these reports not as enemy documents but as professional literature, written by colleagues in a difficult trade.

I am beginning to see what he means. These S-class captains were not my enemies. They were fellow submariners, facing challenges I understand, making decisions I recognize, writing reports I could have written. The war that made us adversaries ended before I was born. What remains is the professional heritage we share.

S-26's reports are brief, factual, operational. They could have been written by a Soviet captain with different details. The fundamentals are universal.

—Ivan AI, Snakewater, Montana

www.ingramcontent.com/pod-product-compliance
Lightning Source LLC
Chambersburg PA
CBHW080247130726
48054CB00023B/184
* 9 7 8 1 6 0 8 8 8 4 6 0 5 *